WITHDRAWN

The New Decade

Bazaine *Dubuffet* *Hajdu* *Manessier* *Pignon*

Richier *Soulages* *Uhlmann* *Werner* *Winter* *Armitage*

Bacon *Butler* *Chadwick* *Scott* *Afro* *Burri*

Capogrossi *Minguzzi* *Mirko* *Appel* *Vieira da Silva*

The New Decade

22 European Painters and Sculptors

edited by Andrew Carnduff Ritchie

with statements by the artists

The Museum of Modern Art

New York

in collaboration with

The Minneapolis Institute of Arts

Los Angeles County Museum

San Francisco Museum of Art

Copyright 1955. The Museum of Modern Art, New York
Printed in the United States of America

Acknowledgments

On behalf of the Trustees of the Museum of Modern Art, New York, The Minneapolis Institute of Arts, the Los Angeles County Museum and the San Francisco Museum of Art, I wish to convey my deepest gratitude to: the artists in the exhibition, for their statements and their cooperation; the collectors, museums and dealers whose generosity in lending has made the exhibition possible and whose names appear on page 107; Mrs. Lilian Somerville and the staff of the British Council for extraordinary help in selecting and securing British loans and artists' statements; Francis J. McEwen for his devoted assistance in securing the statements from French and other artists living in Paris; Dr. Robert E. Schneider for securing artists' statements from Italy; Lester Cooke for obtaining many photographs from Italy; Darthea Speyer for her help and advice; the translators of foreign statements: Margaret Scolari Barr for the Italian; Mme Pierre Chareau for the French; Herwin Schaefer, with the assistance of Robert Motherwell, for the German; Hans van Weeren-Griek for the Dutch; for special assistance in securing loans: Philip James, Sir John Rothenstein, Jean Cassou, W. J. H. B. Sandberg; Margaret Miller and Ellen Mary Jones for research, editing of translations and the preparation of biographical notes on the artists; Jane Sabersky for assistance in German translations; and Alicia Legg for research and secretarial work throughout.

ANDREW CARNDUFF RITCHIE
Director of the Exhibition

Exhibition Dates

The Museum of Modern Art: May 10–August 7, 1955
The Minneapolis Institute of Arts: September 21–October 30, 1955
Los Angeles County Museum: November 21–January 7, 1956
San Francisco Museum of Art: February 2–March 15, 1956

Contents

. . . to adjust the Reason to the phantasmagoria of Life. And, while maintaining the steadfast lapis lazuli within, to have it played upon by every delicate shading of the weather, deepening its azure now and lighting it again in tone with the luminous and magical haze which is tremulous with life. To be magical as Life itself, and as irresponsible: to be lunatic enough to take the hard edge from knowledge, to be irrational enough to temper Justice with Mercy, and to be able to adjust oneself to the changes in intensity which the waxings and wanings of Reality assume in the shimmerings of its cloud— this would be an ideal adjustment and a poetic opposition to outrageous Fortune.

Oliver St. John Gogarty

AS I WAS GOING DOWN SACKVILLE STREET

Foreword

European art and politics are today in a state of flux. In both there are signs of sober hope, which are all the more remarkable when seen against a decade of anxiety, not to say despair. Great powers have suffered defeat or a tremendous diminution of their strength. Many political and artistic leaders are now old or have died in the past few years. Even so, there has been a stirring of ideas that may eventually lead to a more stable, unified continent; and among younger artists there appears to have been a serious reappraisal of pre-war art movements and a searching for new points of departure.

The greatest tensions during the decade have been political. One by-product has been that in art the Communists have sought to steal the term "realism," just as they have sought to appropriate the words "peace" and "democracy." In France most non-Communist painters tend to be abstract, in one way or another. In Italy and West Germany the same is true, and in these two countries the memory of the sentimental, would-be heroic realism of Fascist or Nazi art may have had something to do with their choice of an opposite direction. Britain, on the other hand, with more conservative political and artistic traditions has been less affected by these totalitarian pressures.

It would be foolish to suggest that many painters have turned to some kind of non-objective or non-figurative art only to avoid the social realism of the Communists or the Fascists. The beginnings of abstract art pre-date the Soviet revolution by a number of years. One may speculate, however, that the weakness, even sterility, of most non-Communist figurative painting is in part the result of stronger minded artists having chosen an extreme reactionary or advanced position, leaving the middle ground to become impoverished. This impoverishment is no doubt a great misfortune; but it should surprise no one in a world where the middle ground between ideological extremes becomes daily more difficult to maintain. Among artists of the past decade there are, fortunately, a few embattled eccentrics like Dubuffet and Bacon, who go their own way.

Of the fourteen painters here presented, nine are abstract, in one or another meaning of that ambiguous term. Of the eight sculptors, only one has maintained a purely abstract direction. Some of the others, particularly the British sculptors Butler and Chadwick, while they may have been abstract in their beginnings, are now becoming more interested in the figure in the round. Possibly Henry Moore, who has been the chief inspiration for a revival of sculpture in the United Kingdom, has been responsible for this British trend, if trend it is. However abstract, in an organic sense, some of his sculpture has been, he has recently produced work directly inspired by Greek and Etruscan sculpture. On the Continent, however, while a number of excellent constructivist or abstract sculptors have been produced in this century, something basically figurative in the tradition of sculpture has kept the majority of sculptors within the figurative camp. The middle ground here has not, for some reason, become so impoverished, perhaps because sculpture has not been so exposed to the violent extremes of realism versus abstraction which her sister art has experienced. Sculpture, for one thing, is a more expensive, less mobile medium and does not lend itself as easily as painting does to mass propaganda. Perhaps for these reasons Communist debasement of figurative imagery has had less opportunity to operate. Conversely, it may be significant that in Nazi Germany, which did use sculpture for propaganda purposes, a strong-willed Uhlmann, a political prisoner for two years, maintained his artistic independence by continuing to produce constructions that had no propaganda value whatsoever.

One can only speculate, however, on the reasons why artists today follow one direction or another. Even their statements that follow (all but two published for the first time) give only vague clues as to why they paint or make sculpture as they do. Nevertheless, in reading them one is struck by how much these statements have in common and by the similarity of problems or experience referred to: the rôle that instinct or intuition plays in creation; how much the act of making has to do with discovering what a work will turn out to be; the work of art as an entity; art as an instrument for discovering meaning in the world; the relation of art to the object or the external world; and finally, the most frequent reference, the question of *space*.

Most modern movements have been concerned with the discovery of a space that would be appropriate to our time. The color-defined space of the Fauves, the multiplaned perspective of the Cubists, the metaphysical infinities of the Surrealists—all were spatial revolutions, countering each other and in opposition to the picture-window perspective of the Renaissance. As many of these statements imply, the exploration goes on.

Soulages calls space "a dynamic of the imagination . . . A painting that is really lived . . . measures this space that is really ours by creating its own." For Appel, painting "is a spatial experience, which, nourished by instinct, becomes a living form." Scott tells us that what interests him in the beginning of a picture is "the division of spaces and forms; these must be made to move and be animated like living matter." Vieira da Silva maintains that a painting "in its movements . . . should be like a person and have the tempo of a person's movements." Afro feels that "the substance of my color, the development of my lines create a space which stands for the dimensions of memory." And Capogrossi says that "my ambition is to help men to see what their eyes do not perceive: the perspective of space in which their thoughts move and their actions are born."

These are a few quotations that may help to point up the diversity of attack that is being made on a common problem. A careful reading of the statements as a whole will show a similar casting about for words to express common strivings. And, as so many of the artists complain, words are inadequate to describe the mysterious process of creation or even the finished painting or sculpture.

But however cryptic their language, these "credos" or explanations have more than documentary value. Sometimes expressed with obvious difficulty, sometimes with eloquence, they tell us something of the passion, struggle, adventure and discovery that go into the act of creation. There remains the most important thing of all, the work of art itself.

It should be emphasized that this selection of twenty-two European artists is a personal one. It is exclusive and, inevitably, arbitary. Having said as much, it need hardly be added that the choice was made with deliberation and heart searching. The object has been, however, to present a limited number of artists with from three to five examples of their work, rather than a greater number with but one painting or sculpture apiece. The arrangement is alphabetical according to country and alphabetical within each country.

The artists chosen have all made a special contribution to the art of the past ten years. They have all come into prominence during these post-war years, however long before the war some of them may have studied and striven for recognition.

Not every European country is represented, but then it must be admitted that not every European country has produced distinguished new artists. Why one country rather than another provides a fertile soil for artists must remain an open question. There are answers—sociological, geographical, economic—but none is altogether satisfactory. The enormous element of chance that goes into the making of each one of us is a simple matter compared with the mysterious accident of an artist's birth.

A. C. R.

Bazaine

Jean Bazaine.
Photograph by Ernst Scheidegger

It was no doubt necessary for painting to arrive at a conscious "non-objectivism" in order that we might more clearly understand that man—consciously or not—has never in all his 40,000 years of painting produced a single "objective" picture. And that, since the nature of painting is abstraction, it should be understood that art, figurative or not, has always been abstract.

I am not so sure that it was useful to invent the word *"informel,"* in order to plunge ourselves again into that untamed volcano, that indomitable part that lies concealed in all true art.

It is not only "anti-painting" that reminds us, in terms all too obvious, that a work of art exists only in the degree to which it denies itself, exceeds itself, blasphemes . . .

Never until now has art been more concerned about having a civil status and clearly defined objectives, after having sworn to us that it had undertaken to live dangerously.

So many of the "isms" that have been staking out boundaries for painting over

Earth and Sky. 1950. Oil on canvas,
76¾ x 51¼". Galerie Maeght, Paris

The Flame and the Diver. 1953.
Oil on canvas, 76¾ x 51¼".
Galerie Maeght, Paris

Chicago. 1953. Oil on canvas, 57½ x 45″.
Collection Louis Gabriel Clayeux, Paris

the past fifty years have been often only expressions of an anxious search for clarity, of a timidity that, as it increased, took on an appearance of defiance.

But there is something else, something more important in this defiance. It is the anguish of a man turned in on himself, dispossessed of a world he no longer recognizes. It is his agonized effort to prove to himself again that his existence is inextricably linked to painting, and that he demands violently not to please but to exist.

At the turning point of this fine, vehement story, which has been the pattern of schools or groups in increasing number, the painter of today again finds himself alone and his painting can no longer be labeled. Surely it is time for him to give up the naïve epithet "modern"—and, especially, "avant-garde"—terms which never had the slightest sense, but which were, for too many persons, signs of I don't know what kind of guilty conscience, a need for self-justification.

These are luxuries for which we have paid dearly. Our task is certainly less spectacular than that of our predecessors, but it is no less thankless. Now that so many experiences which were thought to be contradictory are behind us, it is no longer possible to ignore the fact that the vitality of an art resides in the richness of its contradictions, and that the strength of an artist consists in his acceptance of them. Consequently, art has renounced the comfort of the groups that so conveniently help in sharing anxieties and responsibilities: the security of the prohibitionists who limit the hazardous paths of art; the exaltation, so reassuring, of doctrines and manifestoes; the crutches of the "avant-garde." Once again we have the right to be weak on our own.

It rests with us once more to rediscover, by means impossible to foresee, our most interior, most secret visage, that of the external world. To learn patiently again that heat and cold, the space of trees and beasts are not distant or tamed entities, and that this vast world turns within us.

JEAN BAZAINE

JEAN BAZAINE (French). Painter. Born Paris, 1904. Took a degree in literature and studied sculpture before turning to painting in 1924. First one-man show, 1932, attracted interest of Bonnard and Gromaire. One of the founders of the *Salon du Temps Présent*. Organized May, 1941, the first exhibition of modern painting under the German Occupation, *Vingt Peintres de Tradition Française*, Galerie Braun, which included Manessier, Pignon and other young painters. Exhibited regularly in Paris after 1941 in one-man shows or with other artists, principally Villon, Estève, Lapique. Designed three stained glass windows for the church at Assy, 1943–47, and façade mosaic for church at Audincourt, 1951. Has contributed articles on painting to *Nouvelle revue française* and other French journals and published in 1948, *Notes sur la peinture d'aujourd'hui*. Included in the French section of the Venice Biennale, 1948, 1952 and in the São Paulo Bienal, 1951, 1953. Served as a juror at the Carnegie International Exhibition, Pittsburgh, 1952. Lives in Paris.

Jean Dubuffet. Photograph, courtesy Pierre Matisse Gallery

The merit which we Occidental nations attribute to art and the attention lavished on it tend to substitute a specious product which is the counterfeit of art. Too highly honored, art is rarely nowadays a free celebration (to which one would rush even if it were forbidden and probably rush even faster because it is forbidden). It has become, instead, a game of ceremonies which leads it far into alien terrain. Its true and only terrain is rapture and delirium; it is extra-curricular and doesn't belong in the school schedule. To help art regain its place, it should, I believe, be stripped of all the tinsel, laurels and buskins in which it has been decked, and be seen naked with all the creases of its belly. Once disencumbered, it will doubtless begin again to function—to dance and yell like a madman, which is its function, and stop putting on pretentious airs from its professor's chair.

JEAN DUBUFFET

Paris Street with Stealthy Pedestrians.
1944. Oil on canvas, 34¾ x 45¾".
Collection Mr. and Mrs. Charles
Zadok, Milwaukee

Below: *Nude, Olympia.* 1950.
Oil on canvas, 35 x 45¾".
Pierre Matisse Gallery, New York

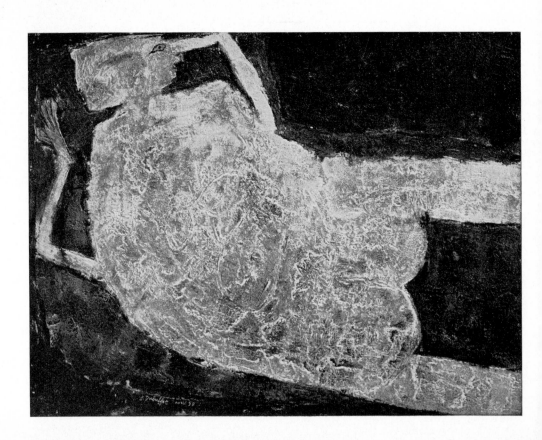

Building Façades. 1946. Oil on canvas, 44⅞ x 57½″. Collection Mr. and Mrs. Samuel A. Marx, Chicago

The Busy Life. 1953. Oil on canvas, 51 x 77″. Owned by the artist

The Tramp. 1954. Oil on canvas, 45½ x 35".
Collection Mr. and Mrs. David M. Solinger, New York

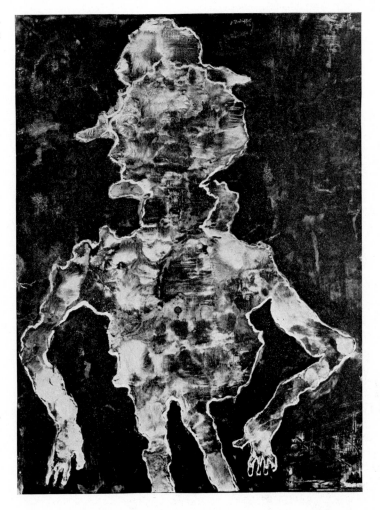

JEAN DUBUFFET (French). Painter. Born Le Havre, 1901. Began painting at 17, studying briefly at l'Académie Julian, Paris. Lived in Montparnasse; read widely in ethnology, paleography, ancient and modern literatures. After seven years gave up painting, became a clerk and later a wine merchant. Has stopped painting and returned to it twice since that time. Unknown as a painter until one-man show after the Liberation of Paris, October, 1944. Worked at lithographs exclusively the following year. After 1945 intensified interest in *l'Art brut,* the work of prisoners, mediums, the insane and other non-professionals. Later formed society to collect and exhibit *l'Art brut.* About 1948, first of several sojourns in North Africa, principally in the Sahara oasis of El Goléa. Visited New York, winter 1952. First one-man exhibition in America, Pierre Matisse Gallery, 1947. Published *Prospectus aux amateurs de tout genre,* 1946; *l'Art brut préféré aux arts culturels,* 1951, and two portfolios of lithographs, *Matière et memoire,* and *Les murs.* Lives in Paris.

Hajdu

Etienne Hajdu.
Photograph by Denise Colomb

The traditional task of the sculptor has always been to re-create from earth, stone or metal the vehicle of his reality. The reality of today, or more precisely my reality, is to be neither "elsewhere" nor "another person" but to open my eyes to the here and now.

This, then, is why I have abandoned the sculpture-object, which by its form and content is incapable of expressing the manifold aspects of life.

I have turned to bas-relief, which allows one to reunite technically many contrary elements and to assure their interaction.

The undulation of the relief can unite form and background. It also gives a spatial sensation without perspective; light makes its way across the surface little by little.

ETIENNE HAJDU

Above: *Soldiers in Armor*. 1953. Sheet copper,
38¾ x 77¼". Galerie Jeanne Bucher, Paris

Portrait Head. 1950. Marble, 18¼" high.
Collection Mme Etienne Hajdu, Paris

Opposite: *The Young Girls.* 1954. Sheet aluminum, 38½ x 66″.
Galerie Jeanne Bucher, Paris

Woman with Braids. 1953. Bronze, 33½″ high.
Collection Mr. and Mrs. Charles Zadok, Milwaukee

ETIENNE HAJDU (French). Sculptor. Born Turda (Rumanian Transylvania), 1907, of Hungarian parents. Encouraged by father to study art. Went to Paris in 1927. For three years studied with Bourdelle, Niclausse, and at the Ecole des Beaux Arts. Left the school after seeing a Léger exhibition in 1930. Same year became a French citizen. After military service traveled in Greece, Crete, Holland. Toured France on bicycle to study Romanesque sculpture. First exhibited with Vieira da Silva and Arpad Szenes at Galerie Jeanne Bucher, 1939. Served in the war; during the Occupation worked as a marble cutter in a factory in the Pyrenees. First one-man exhibition, Paris, 1946. Lives outside Paris in Bagneux.

Manessier

Alfred Manessier. Photograph, courtesy *Arts Digest*

I cannot speak of painting; words are too far removed from colors! When I reread what I have said or what someone has been able to make me say, I nearly always have a feeling of regret, and an impression of total inexactness.

I feel the unity of a certain blue and a certain red, that's all; this is what is important and this is what can't be explained. It is in the realm of feeling. The domain of the intelligence is of another order.

I prefer by far the painter of a good picture to the author of many volumes of theories on the problems of modern art. Let the critics and art historians do their work and let us do ours; our job is to paint, not to explain.

For myself, I paint in response to my desire for harmony and unity, to a renewal of self, reconstructed step by step, towards this world lost from grace. But such painting is far removed from the public, because the public lives in a materialistic world and no longer has need of what I wish to express. This need for harmony and unity is as though asleep and we must watch for an awakening.

Sooner or later the world will once more feel this need. But I believe also that in order to understand our painting, it is necessary that Christianity recover its place in the life of the world; all will be saved if we recover the evangelical spirit, the spirit of childhood. It is natural for a child to feel the harmony between a certain blue and a certain yellow—at least in the first years of its life. But men of today are opposed to

26

Figure of Piety. 1944–45.
Oil on canvas, 57½ x 38¼". Collection
Mr. and Mrs. Charles Zadok, Milwaukee

this feeling; they think only of business, of their cars, etc. . . . and they reject more and more the idea of eternity.

We are living in the time of the Apocalypse, in the time of the end of the world, but we must not be discouraged. We must continue to hope and to work. Perhaps in a few centuries the public and the artist will of necessity feel things in common, unless God intervenes before, which is my ardent wish.

The aged Cézanne, at the end of his life, asked: "Could art be a priesthood?"

ALFRED MANESSIER

The Crown of Thorns. 1950. Oil on canvas,
65 x 38½″. Musée National d'Art Moderne, Paris

Games in the Snow. 1951. Oil on canvas, 28⅞ x 36⅜". Carnegie Institute, Pittsburgh

ALFRED MANESSIER (French). Painter. Born Saint-Ouen, 1911. Spent youth in Abbeville and Amiens. To Paris, 1929. Began painting independently while studying architecture at Ecole des Beaux Arts. After 1935 devoted himself exclusively to painting, studying with Bissière at the Académie Ranson. Broke away from figurative painting. Exhibited later with Bissière and his students, Le Moal, Bertholle and Etienne Martin. Left Paris in 1936 at death of his father. Served in French Army, 1939–40. In 1941 participated in first exhibition of modern painting under the Occupation (organized by Bazaine). Since then has taken part in many group exhibitions in France and abroad. First one-man show, color lithographs, Paris, 1949. Since the war has designed a tapestry for a Dominican convent and stained glass windows for churches in Assy, Bréseux, Basel and Arles-Trinqtaille. Has lived in Paris since 1941.

For the Feast of Christ-The-King. 1952. Oil on canvas, 78 x 59″. Collection G. David Thompson, Pittsburgh

Edouard Pignon

It is necessary, then, to place oneself in a category? . . . Am I figurative, abstract, expressionist, intimist, or any one of those words that the most deadly side of art criticism has so abused as to obscure the entire artistic horizon of the last half century?

I paint because my way of life is to paint. Painting is for me the best road to knowledge, the best means of participating profoundly in the life of the world, the best means of communicating with it.

This world, this nature and this reality are the material with which—or against which —I struggle daily.

I have always been, I am, and I shall always be a painter for whom interior meditation is not possible without contact with reality; a painter for whom the rôle of sifter of reality does not suffice.

However transposed it may be in my painting, nature lives and reigns there and has always reigned there. Each of the themes that I have in turn adopted, after having worked and tested them at length according to my particular method, bears witness to this. I need harbors, olive orchards, nudes or workers, everything that moves and lives passionately under the light of the world. I am no hermit. Though the long solitude of the studio is necessary for me to paint, my life must be constantly immersed in day to day reality, which includes Paris itself, with all its artistic disputes, where ideas are stirred up unceasingly, with its innumerable painters, with Picasso and Léger.

Pignon

No one expects from me a series of profound thoughts on art with a capital A. All I can say is that for me art consists in taking a bit of reality "out of *reality*" (as one would say "out of *nature*"), taking what suits me, then coming to grips with the result of this encounter in my studio. This adds up to nothing original, you will say. But then why make a painter express himself in words? The more he does so the less does he deliberate about what to put down on his canvas, the less attention he directs to what he has chosen to paint; it is the canvas, once begun, which guides him. It is only when he lets himself be carried away without resistance in the direction indicated by his picture that he realizes either what he had hoped to do, or even something he did not expect, and suddenly there are opened up to him new vistas and, at the same time, new kinds of space, in the technical meaning of the word.

Olive Tree at Sunset. 1953. Oil on canvas, 51 x 76¾". Collection Thomas Olsen, Oslo

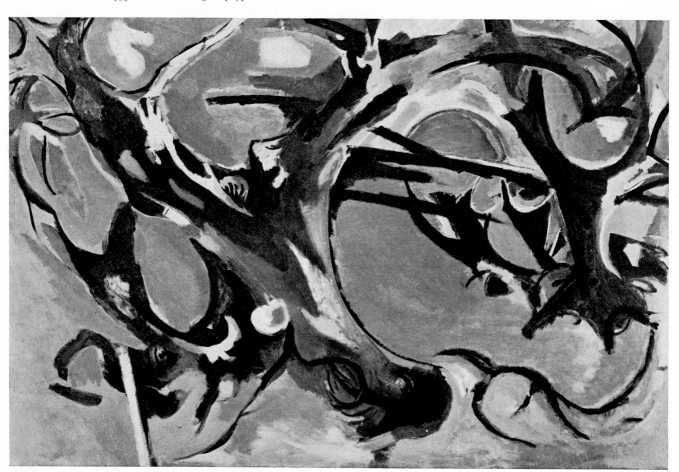

Black Nude. 1953. Oil on canvas, 51 x 76¾". Collection Thomas Olsen, Oslo

My researches, like those of many others, belong to this cycle. They tend to open up on the canvas the new space of our time. There are so many spaces: Romanesque, Renaissance, Impressionist, Cubist, all dead, and surmounting them is the space that I am looking for, along with everyone else. This space will not leave its verticality to the image, it will not pierce the canvas, it will not evaporate in light, it will not play geometrically with the face and the profile.

The problem of space in painting is the basis of all my researches, of all my battles against and with reality.

EDOUARD PIGNON

33

EDOUARD PIGNON (French). Painter. Born Marles-les-Mines, 1905. Son of a miner. From the age of 15 worked in the mines and in the building trades. Military service Syria, 1925–26. Settled in Paris, 1927; earned living in various ways (as comedian, foreman in Renault plant, etc.) and studied drawing and sculpture in night classes, 1928, 1930–34. Knew Frans Masereel and later Léger. Before the war executed a large decorative panel for the Paris Exposition, 1937, and a mural for a school in Creil, 1939. Participated with Bazaine, Manessier and others in *Vingt Peintres de Tradition Française,* May, 1941, first exhibition of modern painting under the Occupation. First one-man show, Galerie René Drouin, Paris, 1946. Since the war sojourns in Collioure and Ostend. Traveled in Sweden, 1946, and Italy, 1949. Included in many international exhibitions: the French sections of the Venice Biennale, 1948, and the São Paulo Bienal, 1951 and 1953. Has illustrated one book of poetry with lithographs, and designed for the theater. Lives in Paris and has worked in Vallauris in a studio lent by Picasso.

Jasmine Pickers. 1954. Oil on canvas, 28¾ x 36¼". Galerie de France, Paris

Germaine Richier.
Photograph by Brassai

How speak of sculpture when the artist dreams of different works, often opposed; of his personal work, his own works (why hide it?); of the evolution of sculpture? One asks then the artist to be at the same time a critic, on the plane of language.

Autonomous, sculpture obeys laws at once immutable and modified. These laws make a basic technique necessary; it is impossible to improvise in this field. Examined in this connection (which is not dependence), sculpture belongs to the exact, modern sciences. In the process of giving movement to form, on the other hand, a more creative activity is involved.

Everything depends, in certain cases, on proposed relationships (let us suppose that they are established) between the volume, constructed little by little, and what is called the subject. Although unpremeditated, my "subjects" belong to the world of metamorphosis (*Storm, Man of the Forest*); to this animal that is more than animal, within or after the form (*The Mantis*)—the fantastic creatures of an age that we are incapable of recognizing, but which is ours, since the world of forms intervenes unceasingly during our research and observation. Everything depends on the drama perceived. In fact, it is discovered along the way, from the elements. Exact science, human science—the

Diabolo (Large version). 1949. Bronze, 66″ high.
Allan Frumkin Gallery, Chicago

The Water. 1952. Bronze, 57″ high. Owned by the artist

value of sculpture depends on this dual relationship, between observation and creation; between truth and imagination.

Finally, sculpture is a *lieu,* an entity, a synthesis of movements. I do not know if *Tauromachy* evokes the bull ring, but no form, it seems to me, can be separated from its world, from the elements. It is then something other than an image. Even in the portrait bust (which has its laws), I do not isolate a character, the individual. This is a *being* which the sculptor takes by surprise. And the being seized takes on value from its organic density, from the play and interaction of the elements. If one were to speak of sculpture's superlative function, one would say that it rediscovers the meaning of the world and of the hybrid.

GERMAINE RICHIER

37

Tauromachy. 1953. Bronze, 45″ high.
Owned by the artist

GERMAINE RICHIER (French). Sculptor. Born Grans near Arles, 1904. From 1922–25 attended Ecole des Beaux Arts in Montpellier, then settled in Paris where she studied with Bourdelle until 1929. Began exhibiting in Paris in 1934. Spent war years in Zurich. Exhibited jointly with Marini and Wotruba at the Kunsthalle, Basel, 1945. Returned to Paris in 1946. Since the war has been represented in several important international sculpture exhibitions: the Venice Biennale, 1948, 1952, 1954 and São Paulo Bienal, 1951, 1953. Bronze crucifix, executed for church in Assy, removed in 1951 after controversy and later replaced through papal intervention. First one-man exhibition in America, Allan Frumkin Gallery, Chicago, 1954. Lives in Paris.

Pierre Soulages. Photograph by Arnold Newman

When I paint I have no ideas about painting; forms, colors, materials and their syntheses are beyond words, inexpressible. What I can write is just an attempt—only an attempt—at comprehension of what affects me and what is for me a necessity.

I believe that a painter reveals more of himself in the way he works, by the description he can give of it, than by stating his intentions or his ideas on art.

As for me, I have not what one would call an imaginary model nor even a precise intention; I work, guided by an inner impulse, a longing for certain forms, colors, materials, and it is not until they are on the canvas that they tell me what I want. It is what I do that teaches me what I am seeking. It is only by painting that I learn what I am seeking.

It is from this sequence of desires, this series of impulses that are almost instinctive, and the interrogation of the combined forms, colors and materials brought to me by these impulses, that the picture is born.*

The world is not absent from a painting because its image—one of its images—is absent from the canvas.

If by figuration a painting introduces point by point connections with the world, non-figurative painting introduces other relationships. For spectator and painter alike,

* From an interview over Radiodiffusion Nationale, June, 1950

January 10, 1951. Oil on burlap, 57½ x 38¼".
The Museum of Modern Art, New York, acquired
through the Lillie P. Bliss Bequest

December 29, 1951. Oil on canvas, 31⅞ x 51¼″. Hillman Periodicals, Inc., New York

the world is not looked at any more, but lived; it has entered into the experience they possess. This experience is tested by the notations which are made and unmade on the canvas.

Thus the picture deprived of representation is invested by the world and owes its meaning to it.*

Because painting is an adventure into the world, it gives the world meaning. Because painting is a poetical experience, it transfigures the world. This metaphor cannot be reduced or impaired by any of the elements of the circumstances of painting, with which there is often a tendency to confuse it.**

Space is a dynamic of the imagination; there is no sense in impoverishing poetry, I mean painting, by denying its significance.

A painting that is really lived, with no arbitrary constraint, no artificial *parti pris,* measures this space that is ours precisely by creating its own.

If my experience as spectator is to be believed, it matters very little to me to know the formula, if one exists, that explains the space of Romanesque painters, of Piero

* From the review *Cimaise,* November, 1953   ** Catalogue of the Salon de Mai, May, 1951

Soulages

October 10, 1952. Oil on canvas, 35 x 45⅝". Collection Mr. and Mrs. Walter Ross, New York

della Francesca, of van Gogh, or of any other. What moves one is to see how these painters got involved in a total human experience, how space or any other element impossible to disconnect from their painting, participates in their poetics, in their style. All this testifies to their humanity and to ours, exalts us, and becomes ours when we look at and delight in one of their pictures.*

PIERRE SOULAGES (French). Painter. Born Rodez, in southern France, 1919. Began painting after finishing high school (lycée). Visited Paris briefly in 1938 where he saw his first Picassos. Served in French Army, 1939–40. Spent the Occupation in central France working as a farmer. In 1946 settled in Paris; began working in abstract style the following year. First one-man show Galerie Lydia Conti, Paris, 1949; others in Copenhagen, 1951; Munich, 1952; and New York, 1954, Kootz Gallery. Has designed for the ballet, 1949, and the theater, Louis Jouvet, 1951. Since 1950 has traveled in Europe, and has been represented in the French sections of the Venice Biennale, 1952, and the São Paulo Bienal, 1953. Lives in Paris.

* From an informal lecture at the Collège de Philosophie, April 27, 1953

April 3, 1954. Oil on canvas, 77 x 52".
Kootz Gallery, New York

Uhlmann

Hans Uhlmann.
Photograph by Ewald Gnilka

The meaning of constructing and forming—the act of creation—this special way of life —is to me the greatest possible freedom. It also means freedom from private feelings (but not without strong feelings) and this also means to be free from dulling tendencies of a didactic or moralizing nature. This is the condition of a man who creates something and is nevertheless astonished when he makes hoped-for discoveries. Many incidents may have prepared this condition, experiences of all kinds, as well as a process of change and purification difficult to demonstrate—a process to which emotion, both conscious and subconscious, contributes. Important to me are the entirely spontaneous drawings which have to be jotted down, mostly without any thought of translation into sculptural terms. I want to create sculpture in a similarly spontaneous way. In sculpture one has to cope with the resistance of the material and of time; and the sense of order, artistic taste, and sculptural thinking must be alert. Sometimes it is important to prepare the right moment for the "spontaneous" and the life-giving element, even in the course of the work itself. My work in metal (since about 1935) has been done directly in the material. I make "spatial" sculpture, which is more than merely three-dimensional sculpture, in which matter seems to have been overcome in much the same way that a dancer, flying across the stage, appears to deny the laws of gravity, and by his apparently effortless performance makes one forget his years of training. The

44

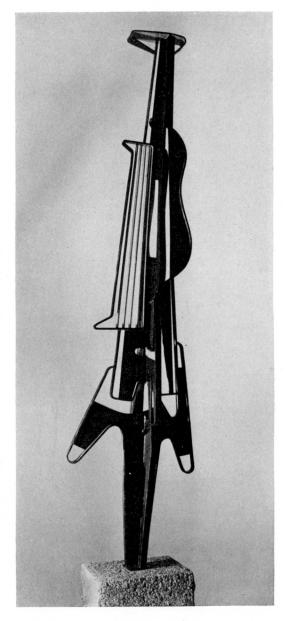

Steel Sculpture. 1954. 34⅝″ high. Owned by the artist

Steel Sculpture. 1951. 78¾″ high. Owned by the artist

kind of sculpture I wish to make has led to the use of entirely immaterial forms, including mirrored images and fragments of mirrored images. I am concerned with a sculpture which aims at all the senses and does not give tactile satisfaction only.

To me the entire question of form and content is superfluous, because both concepts are one. Superfluous also is the discussion of the great topic of our time, of "meaning," because where genuine work is done, there is real "meaning."

HANS UHLMANN

HANS UHLMANN (German). Sculptor. Born Berlin, 1900. Trained as an engineer, Berlin Technical University until 1933. Began working as a sculptor in 1925 without formal training. Visited Paris in 1929. First one-man show, 1930, Galerie Gurlitt, Berlin; exhibited in 1933 with the November Group. Forbidden by the Nazis to exhibit, 1933–45; political prisoner, 1933–35. After his release, forced to earn living as an engineer. First metal constructions in sheet metal and wire begun at this time but not exhibited until 1945. Has won increasing recognition in Germany since the war. One-man show in 1947, Berlin, Galerie Gerd Rosen. After 1951 exhibited in São Paulo, Lucerne, Amsterdam, London, Venice and Milan; international competition for monument to "The Unknown Political Prisoner," London, 1953. Since 1950 has lived in Berlin where he teaches at the Academy of Fine Arts.

Werner

Theodor Werner.
Photograph by Ewald Gnilka

Works of art are a kind of bulletin on the condition of man; his state of being, his participation in life and his dangerous alienation from life.

Man seeks man.

The creative is the compass with which he navigates around the cliffs of one-sided rationalization, mechanization, and around the dangers of becoming barren, empty and a mass man.

Increasing secularization of the Christian idea has dissolved the inner hierarchy of classical composition. The medium of expression now claims equality, and on the basis of its inherent laws it demands authority over creative freedom. Freedom—an imaginary phase-space, the extent of which depends on the dynamics of the creative courage to experiment. For decades the plastic means were re-examined for their evocatory powers, for possible new combinations.

Today the objective is the primacy of the capacity to organize, the primacy of the creative act, producing a new synthesis of means in order to arrive at form by way of individual movements. This means achievement of the metaphysical quality for all work and not only for the work of art.

Homo sapiens struggles for his existence. He can only survive through existing.

Only with the gentle force of the creative act will he master reality.

THEODOR WERNER

48

Vanished (Verschollenes). 1951. Oil on canvas, 39¼ x 31¾". Galerie Ferdinand Möller, Cologne

Prehistoric. 1952. Varnished gouache
on paper, 27½ x 35″.
Collection Mrs. Heinz Schultz, New York

Below: *Venice.* 1952. Oil and tempera
on canvas, 32 x 39⅜″. The Museum
of Modern Art, New York,
gift of Mrs. Gertrud A. Mellon

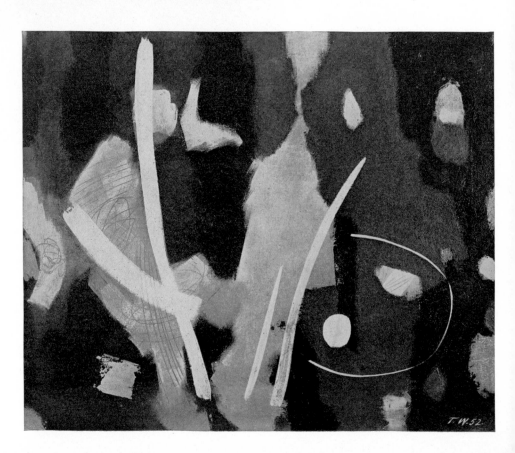

Separation (Loslösung). 1952. Oil on canvas,
39½ x 32″. Owned by the artist

THEODOR WERNER (German). Painter. Born Württemberg, 1886. Studied at Stuttgart Academy,
1908–09. Travel in Germany, Italy and Holland, and yearly visits to Paris, 1909–14. Served in
World War I; lived near Stuttgart, 1919–29, where he had exhibited since 1911. Worked for
five years in Paris, 1930–35; associated with *Abstraction-Creation* group, came to know Carl
Einstein, Braque, Arp and Miro. Visited Italy, Spain, England and United States. Lived
in Potsdam, 1935–45; remained virtually unknown in Germany outside of Stuttgart, though
included in international exhibition, Jeu de Paume Museum, Paris, 1937. After the war moved
to the Western Sector, Berlin. Recognition in Germany dates from one-man exhibition, Gerd
Rosen Gallery, 1947. Executed mural for the Academy of Music in Berlin, 1954. First one-man
exhibition in America, Grace Borgenicht Gallery, New York, 1954.

Winter

Opposite: *Elevation*. 1951. Oil on canvas, 53¼ x 57⅜". Carnegie Institute, Pittsburgh

Fritz Winter. Photograph by Johanna Schmitz-Fabri

My creative work is *not* based on the assumption that the artistic means of painting are exhausted by the reproduction of the visually comprehended world.

The artistic means of color, line and form have an existence and value of their own which permit the creation of new visual conditions outside of the optically perceptible world; new conditions which lie both within and beyond the present optical world.

The artistic substance of a work of art is contained in itself as a separate essence with its own order. It is a part and a whole at the same time: a whole in its pictorial statement; a part in its correspondence to the parallel world of natural law. All creative work is an expression of human experience and understanding. My experience has taught me that life forces art to ever-new expressions. I have come to recognize that our time has raised the picture of the visible world to a great symbol of causal order. The latest results of experiment and research in physics, technology and other fields have led to the same transparency of vision which I consider necessary for contemporary art to arrive at new statements. Science and research have laid bare the inner structure and functional processes of nature.

I consider it my artistic aim to seek, through a transparency of vision, the *content* of the *inner structure* of nature and to understand and give form to its workings. The

outer appearance, even though it reveals some of the essential content, does not satisfy me as an image of its essence.

In many phenomena I see corresponding values and identical content because of parallel effects. High and low, dark and light, warm and cold, and many other opposite values are units of content common to everything in varying degrees. The resulting motion leads to change—to which everything is subject.

It is my aim to bring the creative means at my disposal—color, line, form—back to their own unique qualities and to use them in all their purity. By and through these means the expression of experience should become possible with an organic relatedness; in other words, it should be possible in this way to disclose the values of color, line and form and their functioning.

FRITZ WINTER

Winter

Tensions (Spannungen). 1952.
Oil on burlap, 43¼ x 45¼″.
Galerie Ferdinand Möller, Cologne

FRITZ WINTER (German). Painter. Born Altebögge, in the Ruhr Valley, 1905; eldest son of a coal miner. Trained as an electrician and worked also as miner. Began drawing after seeing work of van Gogh. Studied on scholarship at Bauhaus, 1927–30. Of his teachers, Klee exerted the strongest influence. Taught, 1931, at Teacher's Academy, Halle. Prohibited by the Nazis from exhibiting after 1933; earned living as an artisan. Served ten years in German Army, 1939–45, on Polish and Russian fronts; 1945–49 prisoner of war, Siberia. Work included in post-war exhibitions in Germany before his release. One-man show, 1950, Munich and five other German cities. National recognition, 1951: participated in first exhibition of revived Deutscher Künstlerbund, Berlin; retrospective exhibitions, Munich and Hanover. Since the war has visited France, Italy and Switzerland. First one-man exhibition in America, Hacker Gallery, New York, 1952. Lives in Diessen am Ammersee, near Munich.

Above: *Quiet Sign.* 1953. Oil on canvas,
45 x 57½″. Curt Valentin Gallery,
New York

Approaching (Kommendes). 1954.
Oil on burlap, 37⅞ x 47⅝″.
Collection Nelson A. Rockefeller, New York

Armitage

Kenneth Armitage. Photograph by Ida Kar

I like sculpture to look as if it had happened, and to express an idea as simply as possible. The moment when the work just sufficiently conveys the idea is the time also to finish, as further effort only neutralizes. Uniform overworking or resolving closes in the sculpture so that it becomes imprisoned behind its own stiff façade and is less comfortable in relation to its environment and external space. I like art to be concerned with the intensity of the moment. For this reason I find especially appealing, generous and even tragic, those arts which exist only at the time of their creation and are unlikely to be repeated in the same way again—the great dancers, instrumentalists, singers, cooks, bullfighters and storytellers.

I believe that art is something shared among all of us and feel almost apologetic for the effort and specialization involved in its production. Partly because of this I have felt obliged to give very simple and even frivolous titles to works which have meant rather more to me than their titles suggest.

I find most satisfying work which derives from careful study and preparation but which is fashioned in an attitude of pleasure and playfulness; or work which is supported by the artist's accumulated experience and knowledge, adapted to the idea of the moment, and carried out with the risk and tension of tightrope walking. I prefer using fugitive materials where the work of the moment is final, and a state of urgency is set up by the medium itself.

56

It is always impressive when out of hundreds of known faces a friend can be recognized immediately at even considerable distances. By observing others all our lives we are able to interpret every nuance of shape as a visible indication of character and we all develop shape preference to some degree. Thus sculpture when figurative is more complex than when it is abstract. Although I believe the single human figure is the traditional and familiar standard by which we can best assess ourselves and others, for some time I have been working more with groups than with single figures.

The flatness in much of my recent work was the result of several interests, but mostly it was a device by which I could achieve area without actual bulk. I did not want a skin covering an unknown interior like the 'lump' sculpture characteristic of pre-war work in which the surface had no physical relation to the interior structure, but rather I wished to make objects in which the formation of the bulk could easily be seen as well as the means by which they stood upright. In addition to evoking emotional and

Family Going for a Walk. 1951.
Bronze, 29″ high.
The Museum of Modern Art,
New York, acquired through
the Lillie P. Bliss Bequest

Standing Group II. 1952. Bronze (cast 1954), 41¼″ high. Owned by the artist

Square Figure, Relief. 1954. Bronze, 42 x 27½″. Owned by the artist

Seated Group Listening to Music. 1952. Bronze, 49″ long. Bertha Schaefer Gallery, New York

sculptural experiences, I wanted the object to take its place sympathetically in the ordered human world. The human range of vision is concerned with the baroque textural configuration with which the Earth's form is camouflaged. Gravity stiffens this world we can touch and see with verticals and horizontals—the movement of water, railways and even roads, our canals following the 300 ft. contour, architecture and engineering. We walk vertically and rest horizontally, and it is not easy to forget North, South, East, West and up and down.

KENNETH ARMITAGE

KENNETH ARMITAGE (British). Sculptor. Born Leeds, 1916. Studied Leeds College of Art, 1934–37; Slade School, London, 1937–39. Formerly on staff of Bath Academy of Art; awarded Gregory Fellowship in Sculpture, Leeds University, 1954. First one-man exhibition, Gimpel Fils, London, 1952. Exhibited Venice Biennale, 1952; Salon de Mai, Paris, 1953; 2nd International Exhibition of Open-Air Sculpture, Varese, Italy, 1953; 2nd International Exhibition of Open-Air Sculpture, Antwerp, 1953; Holland Park, sculpture exhibition, London, 1954. First one-man exhibition in America, Bertha Schaefer Gallery, New York, 1954. Lives in London.

Bacon

Francis Bacon. Photograph by Sam Hunter

Everybody has his own interpretation of a painting he sees. I don't mind if people have different interpretations of what I have painted.

[Art is a] method of opening up areas of feeling rather than merely an illustration of an object.

The object is necessary to provide the problem and the discipline in the search for the problem's solution.

A picture should be a re-creation of an event rather than an illustration of an object; but there is no tension in the picture unless there is the struggle with the object.

Real imagination is technical imagination. It is in the ways you think up to bring an event to life again. It is in the search for the technique to trap the object at a given moment. Then the technique and the object become inseparable. The object is the technique and the technique is the object. Art lies in the continual struggle to come near to the sensory side of objects.*

He [Matthew Smith] seems to me to be one of the very few English painters since Constable and Turner to be concerned with painting—that is, with attempting to make idea and technique inseparable. Painting in this sense tends towards a complete interlocking of image and paint, so that the image is the paint and vice versa. Here the brushstroke creates the form and does not merely fill it in. Consequently, every movement of the brush on the canvas alters the shape and implications of the image. That is why real

* From an interview with *Time,* 1952

Figure in a Landscape. 1946.
Oil on canvas, 56¼ x 50".
The Trustees of the Tate
Gallery, London

painting is a mysterious and continuous struggle with chance—mysterious because the very substance of the paint, when used in this way, can make such a direct assault upon the nervous system; continuous because the medium is so fluid and subtle that every change that is made loses what is already there in the hope of making a fresh gain. I think that painting today is pure intuition and luck and taking advantage of what happens when you splash the stuff down.*

* From a tribute to Matthew Smith, published in Smith retrospective exhibition catalogue, Tate Gallery, 1953

Dog. 1952. Oil on canvas,
78¼ x 54¼".
The Museum of Modern Art,
New York

Study after Velasquez' Portrait of Pope Innocent X.
1953. Oil on canvas, 60⅛ x 46½". Collection
Mr. and Mrs. William A. M. Burden, New York

I would like my pictures to look as if a human being had passed between them, like a snail, leaving a trail of the human presence and memory trace of past events, as the snail leaves its slime. I think the whole process of this sort of elliptical form is dependent on the execution of detail and how shapes are remade or put slightly out of focus to bring in their memory traces.

FRANCIS BACON

FRANCIS BACON (British). Painter. Born Dublin, 1910; spent youth in Ireland. Has since lived in England. Practically self-taught. Virtually unknown as painter until about 1945. First one-man exhibition, Hanover Gallery, London, 1949. Visited Africa, 1952. First one-man exhibition in America, Durlacher Brothers, New York, 1953. Exhibited Venice Biennale, 1954. Lives in London, and spends part of each year in Monte Carlo.

Study of a Baboon. 1953.
Oil on canvas, 78 x 54".
Collection Mr. and Mrs.
James Thrall Soby,
New Canaan, Connecticut

Reg Butler. Photograph by Ida Kar

Propositions about art are concerned with art that has already been manifested; the working artist's world is that of works as yet unborn.

The "right" way to make sculpture is by making sculpture.

I make sculpture to discover what kind of sculpture I am going to make. I prefer to spend my time looking for a sculpture that "works" rather than making rules to fetter my future.

Looking for a sculpture is like trying to find the hub of a wheel. Often when one thinks one has found the hub—one is still along a spoke! Often one runs right through the hub and out along another spoke!

If you travel outwards along a spoke *away* from the hub you come towards the sterile world of the academic art systems: "realism," "non-figuration," "the museum fragment."

Art which packs a punch is *always near the hub:* is a fusion of a multitude of strands.

Finding "active" verbal equivalents for plastic manifestations is the writer's excitement, not the working artist's.

The great "truths" about art seem, in the studio, either to be lies or monumental truisms.

But, art *is* artificial!

REG BUTLER

Girl and Boy. 1950–51. Forged and welded iron, 6′9″ high.
The Arts Council of Great Britain

Oracle. 1952. Forged and cast bronze, 6′1″ long. The Museum of Modern Art, New York

Girl with a Vest. 1953–54. Shell bronze, 67½″ high.
Collection Nelson A. Rockefeller, New York

Manipulator. 1954. Shell bronze, 67″ high.
Collection G. David Thompson, Pittsburgh

REG BUTLER (British). Sculptor. Born Buntingford, Hertford-shire, 1913. Trained as architect. Practiced as architect, 1937–50. During World War II worked as blacksmith. Turned to sculpture in 1944. First one-man exhibition, Hanover Gallery, London, 1949. Awarded Gregory Fellowship in Sculpture, Leeds University, 1950. Exhibited Venice Biennale, 1952, 1954; international competition for monument to "The Unknown Political Prisoner," London, 1953 (Grand Prizewinner). First one-man exhibition in America, Curt Valentin Gallery, 1955. Lives in Berkhamsted, Hertfordshire.

Chadwick

Lynn Chadwick. Photograph by Ida Kar

If I look back on my work over a period of years, I can see a development from mobiles and constructions, on to beaten shapes with limbs and connections, to the solid forms on which I'm now working. It seems there has been a deliberate continuity, as if the mobiles had been a research into space and volume (separate parts free in space), and the constructions had been a way of joining the parts together, fixing them in space to make forms, and that these constructions have become armatures for the solid shapes —the iron frames of the construction still delineate the mass and act as lines of tension.

But of course it didn't seem like that to me at the time. With each method I have said what I had to say as well as I could. The actual technique acted as a guide, and gave its character to the work. I emphasize the character which the technique gives. There are limitations—I stress the character imposed by the limitations.

Most of the time I weld in iron, and by this technique I can make constructions or I can make surfaces and shapes—I can straighten or bend or taper, but there are limitations, and I visualize in terms of the possibilities and limitations. I believe that it is necessary for the artist to have feeling for the method in which he works, whatever his medium. I am pleased if the iron forms I make have a sort of organic reality, as if they were the logical expression of the materials which I use. I do not expect much vitality in my work unless this is so.

70

Apart from these practical considerations I do not analyze my work intellectually. When I start to work, I wait till I feel what I want to do; and I know how I am working by the presence or lack of a rhythmic impulse. I think that to attempt to analyze the ability to draw ideas from their subconscious source would almost certainly interfere with that ability.

LYNN CHADWICK

LYNN CHADWICK (British). Sculptor. Born London, 1914. Trained as an architect. After 1946 turned to sculpture constructions. First one-man exhibition, Gimpel Fils, London, 1950. Designed mobile commissioned by Arts Council for Festival of Britain, 1951. Exhibited Battersea Park, London, 1951; Venice Biennale, 1952; international competition for monument to "The Unknown Political Prisoner," London, 1953; Holland Park, sculpture exhibition, London, 1954. Lives in Cheltenham, Gloucestershire.

Barley Fork. 1952. Welded iron, 26½″ high. Collection Nelson A. Rockefeller, New York

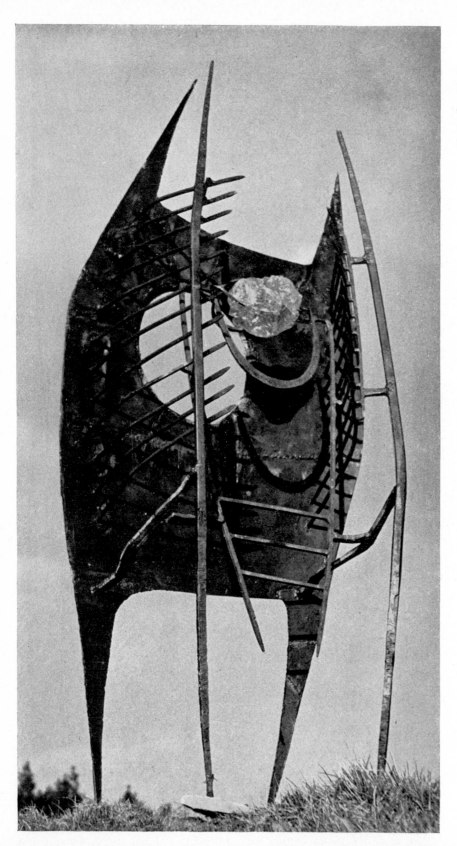

Inner Eye. 1952. Iron with glass, 7′6″ high. Owned by the artist

Opposite: *Two Dancing Figures.* 1954. Iron and composition stone, 71″ high. Owned by the artist

Scott

William Scott. Photograph, courtesy Hanover Gallery

For some time I felt very strongly the need to break from my too conventional arrangements in still-life painting, a conception of space and form which had its roots in the academy of the nineteenth century.

I longed for a freedom from the object or perhaps it was now a desire to divide the spaces of my canvas as I felt and not merely as I knew—the insistence of the objects and their symbolic meaning, wherever I might place them within the picture plane, interfered with my new interest. My problem was to reduce the immediacy of the individual object and to make a synthesis of "objects and space" so that the new conception would be the expression of one thing and not any longer a collection of loosely related objects. While working towards this end my paintings contain greater or lesser degrees of statement of visual fact. Sometimes the object disappears and takes on a new meaning. It is during this moment of transition when I feel I realize most completely my intentions. Apart from the subject, which I can do nothing about, what interests me in the beginning of a picture is the division of spaces and forms; these must be made to move and be animated like living matter. I have a strong preference for primitive and elementary forms and I should like to combine a sensual eroticism with a starkness which will be instinctive and uncontrived.

To have a too clearly conceived idea before beginning a work is for me a constriction; it is in the act of making that the subject takes form, it is in the adding, stretching, taking away and searching for the right and exact statement that a tension is set up. I am horrified at the smart brush or any too easy method of gaining effect. I want to paint what I see but never immediately; there must be a time lapse, "a waiting time" for the visual experience to become involved with all other experience. That is why I paint from memory. I seem to paint the same subject whether it be still life, figure or landscape; there is no escaping, one can develop but never change it. This subject is indefinable, but it is the secret of the picture's success or failure.

WILLIAM SCOTT

Still Life with Colander and Beans. 1948. Oil on canvas, 26 x 32". Collection Howard Bliss, London

Still Life. 1951. Oil on canvas, 45 x 60".
Owned by the artist

Below: *Table Still Life.* 1951. Oil on canvas,
56 x 72". Hanover Gallery, London

Seated Figure. 1954. Oil on canvas, 60 x 30".
Martha Jackson Gallery, New York

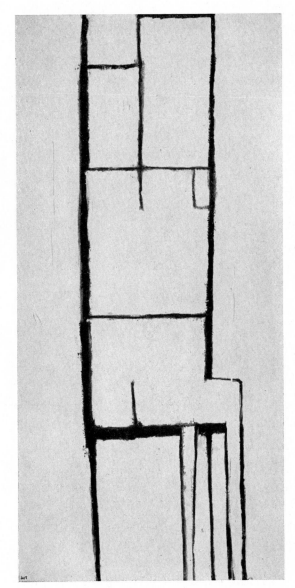

WILLIAM SCOTT (British). Painter. Born Greenock, Scotland, 1913. Spent youth in Enniskillen, Ulster, Ireland. Studied Belfast College of Art and Royal Academy Schools, London. 1937–39 traveled in Italy and France. Elected Sociétaire du Salon d'Automne, Paris, 1939, where he exhibited. First one-man exhibition, Leger Gallery, London, 1942. Retrospective exhibition, Whitechapel Art Gallery, London, 1950. Exhibited São Paulo Bienal, 1953, and Venice Biennale, 1954. Since 1947, Senior Painting Master, Bath Academy of Art. Lives in London.

Afro

Can a pictorial *form* also have value as an *apparition?* Can the rigorously formal organism of a painting contain the lightness, the living breath of an evocation, the leap or shudder of memory? This, for me, is the problem; this is the reason for the constant disquiet that makes me paint. The picture should be an enclosed world; within its limits the drama unfolds; this chessboard spells victory or defeat.

Just yesterday a friend of mine remarked that in my painting forms seem to tremble and move as if possessed by a yearning or a hope for a different ambience—perhaps the one they passed through on their way to concretion?

I cannot decide whether this feeling of animation, of a fluttering breeze, actually invests my images, but often even I feel that the substance of my color, the development of my lines, create a space which stands for the dimensions of memory. Forms open out and take shape as tracks, tracks that have come a long way.

Often I think of myself as a storytelling painter. If my most hidden feelings, my

Dark Chronicle. 1951.
Oil and charcoal
on canvas, 57 x 69". Collection
Mr. and Mrs. Vincent Price, Beverly Hills

memories, my opinions, my intolerances, my faults and terrors can be condensed into the course of a line, into the luminous quality of a tone, then the mysterious flow of my entire being into painting might be willfully reversed so that all my images could go back to the very origins of my life.

This is why I don't avoid the words "dream" or "emotion" or "lyric," all three rejected at present by those who go in for intellectual clarity and awareness of expressive means in contemporary painting.

I like to think that my paintings give forth a sense of hope, a presentiment of dawn. I want them to contain a clear reflection of the world overridden by human passions, but at the same time to unfold with increasing assurance a vast open territory ready for the contests, the sufferings and the celebrations of mankind. I want the sensations of things, the symbols of reality to regain the warmth of a forgotten sentiment within the certainty of pure form. I think painting is getting ready to break away from its exclusive and closely guarded function of instrumental music; it is reaching for new modulations and tones that presage the entrance of the human voice raised in song.

AFRO

Ballet. 1953. Oil and charcoal on canvas, 63 x 35½".
Owned by the artist

AFRO (Italian). Painter. Born Udine, near Venice, 1912. Father painter-decorator. Brother of Mirko. Studied Venice, Florence, Rome. First one-man exhibition, Galleria del Milione, Milan, 1932. Executed murals in Opera Nazionale Balilla, Udine, 1936 (since covered with whitewash) and the Albergo delle Rose, Rodi, 1937. Thereafter turned to still lifes, portraits, landscapes. Member of the Italian Resistance during World War II. Career interrupted during immediate post-war years. In 1948 resumed painting. First one-man exhibition in America, Catherine Viviano Gallery, New York, 1950. Exhibited Venice Biennale, 1952, 1954; São Paulo Bienal, 1951, 1953. Painted murals for the Banca Nazionale del Lavoro, Rome, 1954. Lives in Rome.

Above: *Encounter*. 1954. Oil and charcoal on canvas,
57 x 69". Owned by the artist

Boy with Turkey. 1954. Oil and charcoal on canvas,
49 x 59". Collection Mr. and Mrs. Gordon Bunshaft,
New York

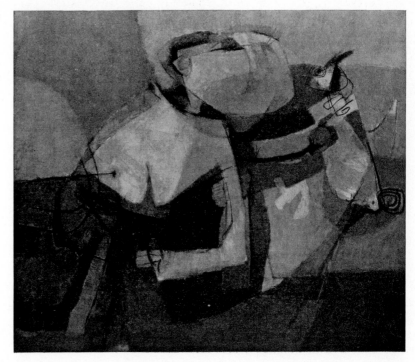

Burri

Alberto Burri. Photograph by Sanford H. Roth

Words are no help to me when I try to speak about my painting.

It is an irreducible presence that refuses to be converted into any other form of expression.

It is a presence both imminent and active.

This is what it stands for: to exist so as to signify and to exist so as to paint.

My painting is a reality which is part of myself, a reality that I cannot reveal in words.

It would be easier for me to say what does *not* need to be painted, what does not pertain to painting, what I exclude from my work sometimes with deliberate violence, sometimes with satisfaction.

Were I master of an exact and less threadbare terminology, were I a marvelously alert and enlightened critic, I still could not verbally establish a close connection with my painting; my words would be marginal notes upon the truth within the canvas. For years pictures have led me, and my work is just a way of stimulating the drive.

I can only say this: painting for me is a freedom attained, constantly consolidated, vigilantly guarded so as to draw from it the power to paint more.

ALBERTO BURRI

Painting. 1951. Oil on canvas, 35¼ x 38⅜″. Collection Mr. and Mrs. Albert Lewin, New York

Burlap and White. 1953. Burlap, cotton on canvas, 59 x 98½". Owned by the artist

ALBERTO BURRI (Italian). Painter. Born Città di Castello (Perugia), 1915. Studied medicine in Perugia. Began painting in 1944 while prisoner of war in Texas. Settled in Rome after the war to devote full time to painting. First one-man exhibition, Galleria Margherita, Rome, 1948. Exhibited Venice Biennale, 1952. First one-man exhibition in America, Allan Frumkin Gallery, Chicago, 1953.

Red and Burlap I. 1954.
Burlap on cotton canvas, 45¼ x 51¼".
Owned by the artist

Below: *All Black II.* 1954. Cotton, silk,
vinavil, glue and paint on celotex,
39½ x 59". Owned by the artist

Capogrossi

Giuseppe Capogrossi.
Photograph by Fotogramma, Milan

I must have been about ten years old when my mother took me with her to visit an institution for the blind. This was in Rome where I was born. In a large room we came upon two children assiduously drawing. Their sheets of paper were jammed with little black signs like a mysterious alphabet, so vibrant and alive that I felt deeply moved, even though at that age I was not interested in art. Somehow, right then, I understood that drawings do not stand necessarily for something *seen* but can also express something within ourselves, perhaps the tension of a human being plunged into reality.

At that precise moment, I think, I felt the call to art, nor was it extinguished by the classical studies my family forced me to undertake for reasons of convention and tradition; in fact my formal education only came to an end when I became a full-fledged doctor of law. At last I could give myself up to painting. For years I was a realistic or representational painter, actually a rather successful one; so much so that many amateurs still mourn my lost talent while some few of the most lenient politely marvel at my conversion to abstract painting.

I, however, am convinced that my painting has not substantially changed; it has only become clearer. From my earliest beginnings I have tried to go beyond the outward appearance of nature; I have always felt that space is a reality within our sentient beings and I have tried to define it. At first I found myself using natural images, comparisons or affinities drawn from the visible world; later I tried to express directly and personally the sense of space I inwardly perceived and came to understand through my everyday actions.

86

I could not forget the blind boy who sought out with his minute and dashing "marks" the form of space which his eyes could not apprehend but which he, nevertheless, intensely felt and lived. Perhaps the formal element that has insistently recurred in my painting since 1949 is a symbol, the footprint of an ancient myth: Michel Seuphor calls it a claw, a hand, a trident, a prong, but then again it may just be a conventional sign as in the Morse Code. At any rate, this formal element turns up again and again but with an irregular frequency and an unaccountable tempo—in life all moments are equal but the texture of time varies. Looking back upon my course I might say that I began with the representation of space, ultimately to achieve the representation of time. The blind boy, my first master, represented as time the space he could not see; yet, despite his infirmity, his life had no less value. My ambition is to help men to see what their eyes do not perceive: the perspective of space in which their thoughts move and their actions are born.

GIUSEPPE CAPOGROSSI

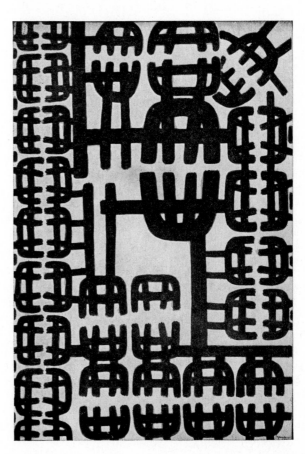

Surface No. 75. 1950. Oil on paper, pasted on canvas, 40⅛ x 28″. Galleria Schneider, Rome

Capogrossi

GIUSEPPE CAPOGROSSI (Italian). Painter. Born Rome, 1900. Studied law. Abandoned this profession for painting. Lived in Paris, 1927–33. Became successful conventional painter. Exhibited with Cagli and Cavelli, Galleria del Milione, Milan, 1933. Began painting in present manner (his so-called "Surfaces") in 1949. Exhibited Venice Biennale, 1948, 1950, 1952 and 1954. Lives in Rome.

Section No. 4. 1953. Oil on canvas, 46⅞ x 38⅝".
Galleria d'Arte del Naviglio, Milan

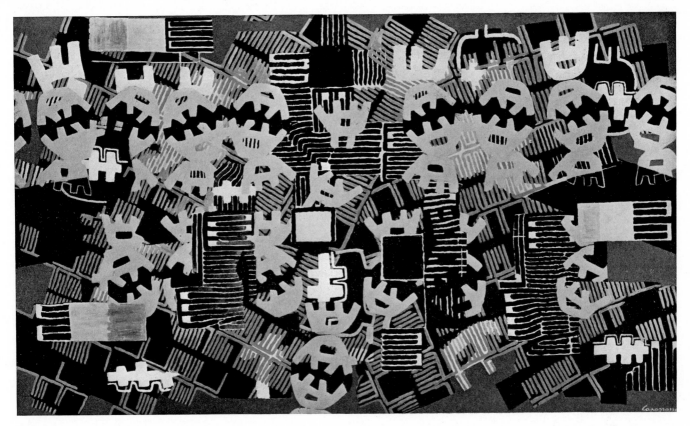

Surface No. 86. 1954. Oil on canvas, 44⅞ x 76¾".
Collection Mr. and Mrs. Harry L. Winston,
Birmingham, Michigan

Surface No. 106. 1954. Oil on canvas, 47¼ x 63"
(oval). Galleria Spazio, Rome

Minguzzi

Luciano Minguzzi.
Photograph, courtesy of the artist

For a sculptor it is hard to put ideas into words, for his natural form of expression is not verbal. I feel reluctant to set down my "credo" because I hesitate to define myself and to classify myself while I am still in the full strength of my production. I can assert or deny things but I cannot set down precisely what I am searching for and pursuing because sometimes I know what I'm after and sometimes I don't. My constant preoccupation is to produce sculpture day by day. Yesterday's plastic problem may be resolved today; its interest then ceases and a new challenge arises. I don't believe that a sculptor's work is instinctive—quite the contrary—I believe firmly in the operation of the mind, in the full acceptance of a cultural background and in self-criticism, all of which should combine with sufficient craftsmanship to enable the sculptor to accomplish his work without pride or presumptuousness.

Sculpture is intrinsically a work of poetry and like poetry it expresses a variety of feelings and moods. All I try to do is to devise the most apposite ways to say what I mean. I reject all devices born of excessive intellectualism because I know, both by instinct and upbringing, that they can never solve the problem in its entirety.

As a Latin I think that the sculptor of today should not confront man in the negativistic position that produced and still produces nothing but formalism and stylization—no, the sculptor should seek out the simple, sincere relationship that served to establish long since the connection between poetry and life.

I must feel in my hands and have before my eyes the assurance of the absolute

Goat. 1951. Bronze, c. 45″ long. Owned by the artist

existence of volumes, of masses, of something that can be touched in all its solid fullness. For my nature and temper this is a necessity far more compelling than the conception of space as an aim in itself.

However, I am not well served by words in my effort to communicate truly and sincerely with men. My works do better and I rely on them for a more profitable and intimate message.

LUCIANO MINGUZZI

LUCIANO MINGUZZI (Italian). Sculptor. Born Bologna, 1911. Son of sculptor. Studied Accademia di Belle Arti, Bologna, and has traveled in nearly all European countries. First exhibited Florence, 1931. Exhibited Venice Biennale, 1934, 1940, 1942, 1948, 1950 and 1952; São Paulo Bienal, 1951; international competition for monument to "The Unknown Political Prisoner," London, 1953. At present, professor at Accademia di Brera, Milan. Lives in Milan.

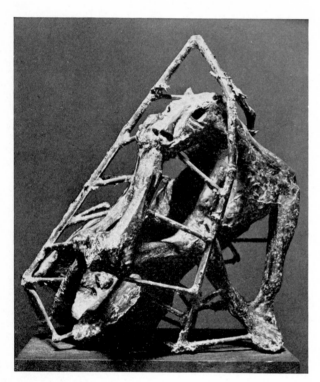

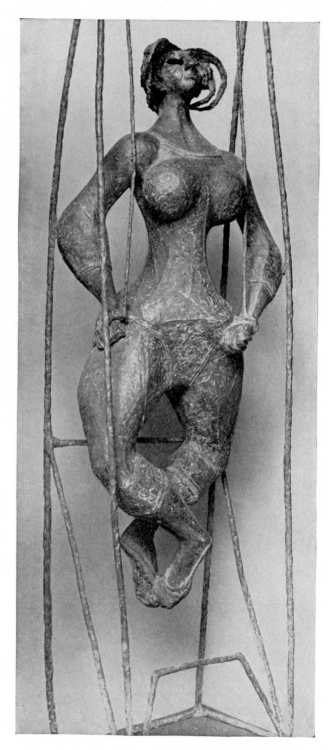

Dog Among Reeds. 1951. Bronze, 27⅛″ high. The Museum of Modern Art, New York, Aristide Maillol Fund

Acrobat on Trapeze. 1953. Bronze, 70⅞″ high.
Owned by the artist

Woman Jumping Rope. 1954. Bronze, 70⅞″ high. Collection Alfons Bach, Stamford, Connecticut

Mirko

Mirko. Photograph by Sanford H. Roth

Before speaking of the plastic idiom of today I should like to draw an analogy with the spoken language. The special character of a people depends upon environment and heredity; it is revealed in that people's ideals and the special meaning it attributes to the various aspects of life. The language of a people stands for a complex system of forms, symbols and words. "And every language is a vast pattern-system, different from others, in which are culturally ordained the forms and categories by which the personality not only communicates, but analyzes nature, notices or neglects types of relationship, channels his reasoning and builds the house of his consciousness."*

Plastic language is equally significant for, within a society, it functions in the same way. Like words, forms acquire a meaning born of the special feeling they evoke; forms are organized into schemes and systems and they derive their power from a common emotive potential. Thought does not need to be expressed in words because it is determined by lines and surfaces, by contrasts of forms, by strident or sweet harmonies, by contrapuntal developments, by precipitations and reconciliations. Plenitude and void become dominant motifs like good and evil, black and white, the conscious and the subconscious.

Like any expressed thought the plastic idiom has a logic all its own with deep roots in man's consciousness: it expresses ideas, arouses feelings, reveals the life of things and men. But the artist of today is not limited in his interpretation of the circumambient world by visual perception; he must learn the laws and the reasons that govern exterior appearance.

* Benjamin Lee Whorf. Quoted by Stuart Chase in *Harper's Magazine,* April, 1954.

 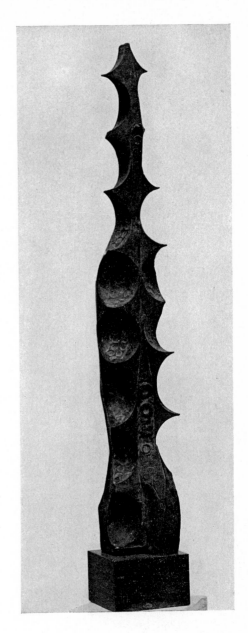

Left: *Hector.* 1949. Bronze,
38¼" high. Collection
Stanley Seeger, Jr., Dallas

Right: *Voices.* 1953.
Bronze, 39" high.
Owned by the artist

The realization of recent scientific achievements gives a special character to the poetry of our time; it sheds light upon unknown worlds and paves the way for new investigations. Contemporary artistic movements appear "modern" thanks to their specialized techniques, but their poetic expressiveness is something quite separate, for it depends on deep and remote motivations, in fact on primordial and subconscious impulses.

Architectonic Element. 1954. Sheet brass,
79 x 39½". Owned by the artist

Chimera. 1955. Bronze, 35½″ high.
Collection Vance Kirkland, Denver.

MIRKO (BASALDELLA) (Italian). Sculptor. Born Udine, near Venice, 1910. Brother of Afro. Studied in Venice, Florence and Monza. First exhibition, Galleria Cairola, Genoa. 1949–50 executed bronze gates for the Ardeatine Cave, Rome, a memorial to 320 Italians killed by the Germans in 1944 in reprisal for death of 32 Germans. First one-man exhibition in America, Catherine Viviano Gallery, New York, 1950. Decorated ceiling for Food and Agriculture Organization Palace in Rome, 1951. Exhibited Venice Biennale, 1952, 1954; international competition for monument to "The Unknown Political Prisoner," London, 1953. Lives in Rome.

Appel

Karel Appel. Photograph by Arnold Newman

Painting is a tangible, sensory experience, an intense "being stirred" by the joy and the tragedy of man.

A spatial experience, which, nourished by instinct, becomes a living form.

I try to capture this tangible reality in paint and in so doing give expression to my times.

KAREL APPEL

KAREL APPEL (Dutch). Painter. Born Amsterdam, 1921. Studied during the war, 1940–43, Royal Academy of Fine Arts, Amsterdam. First exhibited in group show of young painters, Stedelijk (Municipal) Museum, Amsterdam, 1946. One-man shows, Groningen, 1946, and Amsterdam, 1947. In 1948 founded, with Corneille and Constant, Dutch "experimental group" which established contact with other young painters in Denmark and Belgium. Organized first

Child and Beast II. 1951. Oil on canvas, 39¼ x 59¼". Collection Mrs. John D. Rockefeller, 3rd, New York

exhibition of International Experimental Group, Stedelijk Museum, Amsterdam, 1949. From 1949–51 contributed to *Cobra*, the magazine of the international group, and visited Denmark, Belgium, Germany and France, participating in "Cobra" exhibitions in those countries. Executed fresco for coffee shop in Amsterdam City Hall, 1949; mural covered with wallpaper after press controversy. Moved to Paris, 1950. Executed fresco in theater lobby of Stedelijk Museum, Amsterdam, 1951. Has illustrated five books of experimental Dutch and Flemish poetry. Included in Dutch section of São Paulo Bienal, 1953 and Venice Biennale, 1954. First one-man exhibition in America, Martha Jackson Gallery, New York, 1954.

Man and Animals. 1953. Oil on canvas,
43¼ x 55″. Paul Facchetti, Paris

Man with a Brush Cut. 1954. Oil on burlap,
55 x 42½″. Martha Jackson Gallery, New York

Head and Fish. 1954. Oil on canvas, 45 x 76½″. Owned by the artist

Vieira da Silva

Maria Helena Vieira da Silva.
Photograph by Denise Colomb

Each day I am more amazed to "be"; to revolve in space on a globe ...

We are talked to about reality. Everything amazes me, and I paint my amazement which is at the same time wonder, terror, laughter. I would exclude none of my amazement. My desire is to make pictures with many different things, with every contradiction, with the unexpected. I would like to become so agile, so sure of my movements, and of my voice, that nothing could escape me, neither the buoyancy of the birds, the weight of the stones, nor the glow of metal. I would like to observe attentively the strings that pull people forward or hold them back. One should go everywhere, dance, play music, sing, fly, plunge into the depths of the sea, watch lovers, enter factories and hospitals, know by heart many poems, the *code civil,* and the history of nations. But, alas, painting is long, and the days are short.

I see blue cups and a blue-striped tablecloth, a white teapot tinted with blue, a jar of jam shining like a sun.

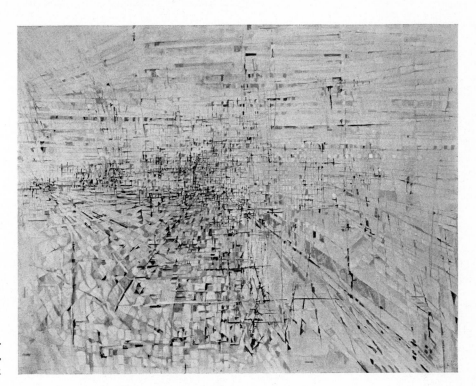

The City. 1948. Oil on canvas, 38¼ x 51".
Collection Mrs. Gilbert W. Chapman,
New York

When I am before my painting and palette, there is a constant effort; a little more white, a little more green, it is too cold, too warm, lines that ascend, that descend, that meet, that part. This means so much in painting and so little in words.

I believe that it is by adding one small brushstroke after the other, toiling like the bee, that a picture is made. A painting must have its heart, its nervous system, its bones and its circulation. In its movements it should be like a person and have the tempo of a person's movements. Looking at it one should feel opposite a being that will keep one company, that will tell one tales, that will give one assurance. For a painting is not escape; it should be a friend who speaks to you, who discovers the hidden treasures within you and around you.

For me, speaking of painting is like playing Blindman's Buff. And while I have been trying to write, I have been haunted by this song:

> *Can you paint a thought? or number*
> *Every fancy in a slumber?*
> *Can you count soft minutes roving?*
> *From a dial's point by moving?*
> *Can you grasp a sigh? or lastly,*
> *Rob a virgin's honour chastely?*

VIEIRA DA SILVA

103

Above: *Iron Bridges*. 1953. Oil on canvas,
45 x 57½". Galerie Pierre, Paris

Theater. 1953. Oil on canvas, 35 x 46¾".
Galerie Pierre, Paris

Nocturnal Space. 1954.
Oil on canvas, 38 x 51″.
Private collection, Paris

MARIA HELENA VIEIRA DA SILVA (Portuguese). Painter. Born in Lisbon, Portugal, 1908. Formal training began at age of 11. To Paris, 1928; studied sculpture with Bourdelle, Despiau; painting with Friesz and Léger. Married the Hungarian painter, Arpad Szenes, 1930. First one-man show, 1933, Jeanne Bucher Gallery, Paris. Worked in Lisbon, c. 1935–36, and spent the war years in Rio de Janeiro, 1940–47. First post-war exhibition, Marian Willard Gallery, New York, 1946. Has exhibited regularly in Paris since 1947 and had one-man shows in Basel, London and Stockholm. Included in the Portuguese section of the Venice Biennale, 1950; and the French section of the São Paulo Bienal, 1953; Venice Biennale, 1954. Among her commissioned works are a tapestry design, 1930; a mural for the Ministry of Education, Rio de Janeiro, 1948; and theater décors for Adamof's *Parodie,* 1952. Lives in Paris.

Catalogue of the Exhibition

LENDERS TO THE EXHIBITION

Afro, Rome; Karel Appel, Paris; Kenneth Armitage, London; Alfons Bach, Stamford, Connecticut; Howard Bliss, London; Mr. and Mrs. Gordon Bunshaft, New York; Mr. and Mrs. William A. M. Burden, New York; Alberto Burri, Rome; Lynn Chadwick, Cheltenham, England; Mrs. Gilbert W. Chapman, New York; Louis Gabriel Clayeux, Paris; Jean Dubuffet, Paris; Mme Etienne Hajdu, Paris; Hillman Periodicals, Inc., New York; Vance Kirkland, Denver; Mr. and Mrs. Albert Lewin, New York; Mr. and Mrs. Samuel A. Marx, Chicago; Luciano Minguzzi, Milan; Mirko, Rome; Thomas Olsen, Oslo; Mr. and Mrs. Vincent Price, Beverly Hills; Germaine Richier, Paris; Mrs. John D. Rockefeller, 3rd, New York; Nelson A. Rockefeller, New York; Mr. and Mrs. Walter Ross, New York; Mrs. Heinz Schultz, New York; William Scott, London; Stanley Seeger, Jr., Dallas; Mr. and Mrs. James Thrall Soby, New Canaan, Connecticut; Mr. and Mrs. David

M. Solinger, New York; G. David Thompson, Pittsburgh; Hans Uhlmann, Berlin; Theodor Werner, Berlin; Mr. and Mrs. Harry L. Winston, Birmingham, Michigan; Mr. and Mrs. Charles Zadok, Milwaukee; The Arts Council of Great Britain, London; The Trustees of the Tate Gallery, London; The Museum of Modern Art, New York; Musée National d'Art Moderne, Paris; Carnegie Institute, Pittsburgh

Galerie Jeanne Bucher, Paris; Paul Facchetti, Paris; Galerie de France, Paris; Allan Frumkin Gallery, Chicago; Hanover Gallery, London; Martha Jackson Gallery, New York; Kootz Gallery, New York; Galerie Maeght, Paris; Pierre Matisse Gallery, New York; Galerie Ferdinand Möller, Cologne; Galleria d'Arte del Naviglio, Milan; Galerie Pierre, Paris; Bertha Schaefer Gallery, New York; Galleria Schneider, Rome; Galleria Spazio, Rome; Curt Valentin Gallery, New York

CATALOGUE   *In dimensions height precedes width*

AFRO. Italian, born 1912

Dark Chronicle. 1951. Oil and charcoal on canvas, 57 x 69". Collection Mr. and Mrs. Vincent Price, Beverly Hills. *Ill. p. 79*

Ballet. 1953. Oil and charcoal on canvas, 63 x 35½". Owned by the artist. *Ill. p. 80*

Encounter. 1954. Oil and charcoal on canvas, 57 x 69". Owned by the artist. *Ill. p. 81*

Boy with Turkey. 1954. Oil and charcoal on canvas, 49 x 59". Collection Mr. and Mrs. Gordon Bunshaft, New York. *Ill. p. 81*

KAREL APPEL. Dutch, born 1921

Child and Beast II. 1951. Oil on canvas, 39¼ x 59¼". Collection Mrs. John D. Rockefeller, 3rd, New York. *Ill. p. 99*

Man and Animals. 1953. Oil on canvas, 43¼ x 55". Paul Facchetti, Paris. *Ill. p. 100*

Head and Fish. 1954. Oil on canvas, 45 x 76½". Owned by the artist. *Ill. p. 101*

Man with a Brush Cut. 1954. Oil on burlap, 55 x 42½". Martha Jackson Gallery, New York. *Ill. p. 100*

KENNETH ARMITAGE. British, born 1916

Family Going for a Walk. 1951. Bronze, 29" high. The Museum of Modern Art, New York, acquired through the Lillie P. Bliss Bequest. *Ill. p. 57*

Seated Group Listening to Music. 1952. Bronze, 49" long. Bertha Schaefer Gallery, New York. *Ill. p. 59*

Standing Group II. 1952. Bronze (cast 1954), 41¼" high. Owned by the artist. *Ill. p. 58*

Square Figure, Relief. 1954. Bronze, 42 x 27½". Owned by the artist. *Ill. p. 58*

FRANCIS BACON. British, born 1910

Figure in a Landscape. 1946. Oil on canvas, 56¼ x 50". The Trustees of the Tate Gallery, London. *Ill. p. 61*

Dog. 1952. Oil on canvas, 78¼ x 54¼". The Museum of Modern Art, New York. *Ill. p. 62*

Study after Velasquez' Portrait of Pope Innocent X. 1953. Oil on canvas, 60⅛ x 46½". Collection Mr. and Mrs. William A. M. Burden, New York. *Ill. p. 63*

Study of a Baboon. 1953. Oil on canvas, 78 x 54". Collection Mr. and Mrs. James Thrall Soby, New Canaan, Connecticut. *Ill. p. 64*

JEAN BAZAINE. French, born 1904

Earth and Sky. 1950. Oil on canvas, 76¾ x 51¼". Galerie Maeght, Paris. *Ill. p. 13*

The Flame and the Diver. 1953. Oil on canvas, 76¾ x 51¼". Galerie Maeght, Paris. *Ill. p. 14*

Chicago. 1953. Oil on canvas, 57½ x 45". Collection Louis Gabriel Clayeux, Paris. *Ill. p. 15*

ALBERTO BURRI. Italian, born 1915

Painting. 1951. Oil on canvas, 35¼ x 38⅜". Collection Mr. and Mrs. Albert Lewin, New York. *Ill. p. 83*

Burlap and White. 1953. Burlap, cotton on canvas, 59 x 98½". Owned by the artist. *Ill. p. 84*

Red and Burlap I. 1954. Burlap on cotton canvas, 45¼ x 51¼". Owned by the artist. *Ill. p. 85*

All Black II. 1954. Cotton, silk, vinavil, glue and paint on celotex, 39½ x 59". Owned by the artist. *Ill. p. 85*

REG BUTLER. British, born 1913

Girl and Boy. 1950–51. Forged and welded iron, 6'9" high. The Arts Council of Great Britain. *Ill. p. 66*

Oracle. 1952. Forged and cast bronze, 6'1" long. The Museum of Modern Art, New York. *Ill. p. 67*

Girl with a Vest. 1953–54. Shell bronze, 67½" high. Collection Nelson A. Rockefeller, New York. *Ill. p. 68*

Manipulator. 1954. Shell bronze, 67" high. Collection G. David Thompson, Pittsburgh. *Ill. p. 69*

GIUSEPPE CAPOGROSSI. Italian, born 1900

Surface No. 75. 1950. Oil on paper, pasted on canvas, 40⅛ x 28". Galleria Schneider, Rome. *Ill. p. 87*

Section No. 4. 1953. Oil on canvas, 46⅞ x 38⅝". Galleria d'Arte del Naviglio, Milan. *Ill. p. 88*

Surface No. 86. 1954. Oil on canvas, 44⅞ x 76¾". Collection Mr. and Mrs. Harry L. Winston, Birmingham, Michigan. *Ill. p. 89*

Surface No. 106. 1954. Oil on canvas, 47¼ x 63" (oval). Galleria Spazio, Rome. *Ill. p. 89*

LYNN CHADWICK. British, born 1914

Barley Fork. 1952. Welded iron, 26½" high. Collection Nelson A. Rockefeller, New York. *Ill. p. 71*

Inner Eye. 1952. Iron with glass, 7'6" high. Owned by the artist. *Ill. p. 72*

Two Dancing Figures. 1954. Iron and composition stone, 71" high. Owned by the artist. *Ill. p. 73*

JEAN DUBUFFET. French, born 1901

Paris Street with Stealthy Pedestrians. 1944. Oil on canvas, 34¾ x 45¾". Collection Mr. and Mrs. Charles Zadok, Milwaukee. *Ill. p. 18*

Building Façades. 1946. Oil on canvas, 44⅞ x 57½". Collection Mr. and Mrs. Samuel A. Marx, Chicago. *Ill. p. 19*

Nude, Olympia. 1950. Oil on canvas, 35 x 45¾". Pierre Matisse Gallery, New York. *Ill. p. 18*

The Busy Life. 1953. Oil on canvas, 51 x 77". Owned by the artist. *Ill. p. 20*

The Tramp. 1954. Oil on canvas, 45½ x 35". Collection Mr. and Mrs. David M. Solinger, New York. *Ill. p. 21*

ETIENNE HAJDU. French, born 1907

Portrait Head. 1950. Marble, 18¼" high. Collection Mme Etienne Hajdu, Paris. *Ill. p. 23*

Soldiers in Armor. 1953. Sheet copper, 38¾ x 77¼". Galerie Jeanne Bucher, Paris. *Ill. p. 23*

Woman with Braids. 1953. Bronze, 33½" high. Collection Mr. and Mrs. Charles Zadok, Milwaukee. *Ill. p. 24*

The Young Girls. 1954. Sheet aluminum, 38½ x 66". Galerie Jeanne Bucher, Paris. *Ill. p. 25*

ALFRED MANESSIER. French, born 1911

Figure of Piety. 1944–45. Oil on canvas, 57½ x 38¼". Collection Mr. and Mrs. Charles Zadok, Milwaukee. *Ill. p. 27*

The Crown of Thorns. 1950. Oil on canvas, 65 x 38½". Musée National d'Art Moderne, Paris. *Ill. p. 28*

Games in the Snow. 1951. Oil on canvas, 28⅞ x 36⅜". Carnegie Institute, Pittsburgh. *Ill. p. 29*

For the Feast of Christ-The-King. 1952. Oil on canvas, 78 x 59". Collection G. David Thompson, Pittsburgh. *Ill. p. 30*

LUCIANO MINGUZZI. Italian, born 1911

Goat. 1951. Bronze, c. 45" long. Owned by the artist. *Ill. p. 91*

Dog among Reeds. 1951. Bronze, 27⅛" high. The Museum of Modern Art, New York, Aristide Maillol Fund. *Ill. p. 92*

Acrobat on Trapeze. 1953. Bronze, 70⅞" high. Owned by the artist. *Ill. p. 92*

Woman Jumping Rope. 1954. Bronze, 70⅞″ high. Collection Alfons Bach, Stamford, Connecticut. *Ill. p. 93*

MIRKO (BASALDELLA). Italian, born 1910

Hector. 1949. Bronze, 38¼″ high. Collection Stanley Seeger, Jr., Dallas. *Ill. p. 95*

Voices. 1953. Bronze, 39″ high. Owned by the artist. *Ill. p. 95*

Architectonic Element. 1954. Sheet brass, 79 x 39½″. Owned by the artist. *Ill. p. 96*

Chimera. 1955. Bronze, 35½″ high. Collection Vance Kirkland, Denver. *Ill. p. 97*

EDOUARD PIGNON. French, born 1905

Olive Tree at Sunset. 1953. Oil on canvas, 51 x 76¾″. Collection Thomas Olsen, Oslo. *Ill. p. 32*

Black Nude. 1953. Oil on canvas, 51 x 76¾″. Collection Thomas Olsen, Oslo. *Ill. p. 33*

Jasmine Pickers. 1954. Oil on canvas, 28¾ x 36¼″. Galerie de France, Paris. *Ill. p. 34*

GERMAINE RICHIER. French, born 1904

Diabolo (Large version). 1949. Bronze, 66″ high. Allan Frumkin Gallery, Chicago. *Ill. p. 36*

The Water. 1952. Bronze, 57″ high. Owned by the artist. *Ill. p. 37*

Tauromachy. 1953. Bronze, 45″ high. Owned by the artist. *Ill. p. 38*

WILLIAM SCOTT. British, born 1913

Still Life with Colander and Beans. 1948. Oil on canvas, 26 x 32″. Collection Howard Bliss, London. *Ill. p. 75*

Table Still Life. 1951. Oil on canvas, 56 x 72″. Hanover Gallery, London. *Ill. p. 76*

Still Life. 1951. Oil on canvas, 45 x 60″. Owned by the artist. *Ill. p. 76*

Seated Figure. 1954. Oil on canvas, 60 x 30″. Martha Jackson Gallery, New York. *Ill. p. 77*

PIERRE SOULAGES. French, born 1919

January 10, 1951. Oil on burlap, 57½ x 38¼″. The Museum of Modern Art, New York, acquired through the Lillie P. Bliss Bequest. *Ill. p. 40*

December 29, 1951. Oil on canvas, 31⅞ x 51¼″. Hillman Periodicals, Inc., New York. *Ill. p. 41*

October 10, 1952. Oil on canvas, 35 x 45⅝″. Collection Mr. and Mrs. Walter Ross, New York. *Ill. p. 42*

April 3, 1954. Oil on canvas, 77 x 52″. Kootz Gallery, New York. *Ill. p. 43*

HANS UHLMANN. German, born 1900

Steel Sculpture. 1951. 78¾″ high. Owned by the artist. *Ill. p. 45*

Steel Sculpture. 1954. 34⅝″ high. Owned by the artist. *Ill. p. 45*

Steel Sculpture. 1954. 78¾″ high. Owned by the artist. *Ill. p. 47*

Winged Insect. 1954. Steel, 23⅝″ high. Owned by the artist. *Ill. p. 46*

MARIA HELENA VIEIRA DA SILVA. Portuguese, born 1908

The City. 1948. Oil on canvas, 38¼ x 51″. Collection Mrs. Gilbert W. Chapman, New York. *Ill. p. 103*

Iron Bridges. 1953. Oil on canvas, 45 x 57½″. Galerie Pierre, Paris. *Ill. p. 104*

Theater. 1953. Oil on canvas, 35 x 46¾″. Galerie Pierre, Paris. *Ill. p. 104*

Nocturnal Space. 1954. Oil on canvas, 38 x 51″. Private collection, Paris. *Ill. p. 105*

THEODOR WERNER. German, born 1886

Vanished (Verschollenes). 1951. Oil on canvas, 39¼ x 31¾″. Galerie Ferdinand Möller, Cologne. *Ill. p. 49*

Prehistoric. 1952. Varnished gouache on paper, 27½ x 35″. Collection Mrs. Heinz Schultz, New York. *Ill. p. 50*

Separation (Loslösung). 1952. Oil on canvas, 39½ x 32″. Owned by the artist. *Ill. p. 51*

Venice. 1952. Oil and tempera on canvas, 32 x 39⅜″. The Museum of Modern Art, New York, gift of Mrs. Gertrud A. Mellon. *Ill. p. 50*

FRITZ WINTER. German, born 1905

Elevation. 1951. Oil on canvas, 53¼ x 57⅜″. Carnegie Institute, Pittsburgh. *Ill. p. 53*

Tensions (Spannungen). 1952. Oil on burlap, 43¼ x 45¼″. Galerie Ferdinand Möller, Cologne. *Ill. p. 54*

Quiet Sign. 1953. Oil on canvas, 45 x 57½″. Curt Valentin Gallery, New York. *Ill. p. 55*

Approaching (Kommendes). 1954. Oil on burlap, 37⅞ x 47⅝″. Collection Nelson A. Rockefeller, New York. *Ill. p. 55*

Selected Bibliography

The reader is referred to the standard indexes for specific articles on the twenty-two artists in the exhibition, and to the Library catalogue for individual citations in foreign sources. References below are either general or national, and are necessarily limited to books and substantial articles.

BERNARD KARPEL, *Librarian of the Museum*

GENERAL REFERENCES

LES AMIS DE L'ART (PARIS). Pour et Contre l'Art abstrait. 58p. ill. Paris, Arte Una, 1947. *Cahier no.11. Includes Bazaine, Manessier and others.*

ART D'AUJOURD'HUI (BOULOGNE). June 1949–Dec. 1954. *Excellent international magazine, with emphasis on French activities. Special numbers on sculpture, collage, avant-garde in Italy, Germany, Great Britain, etc. Absorbed 1955 by "Aujourd'hui," also edited by André Bloc.*

BAZAINE, JEAN. Notes sur la Peinture d'Aujourd'hui. 69p. Paris, Floury, 1948.

CAHIERS D'ART (PARIS). 1926–current. *Periodical edited by Christian Zervos. Basic review of recent European art; occasional special numbers, e.g. Italy, no.1, 1950; articles on Vieira da Silva no.2 1949, Richier, Hajdu (June 1953), etc.*

DIEHL, GASTON, ed. Les Problèmes de la Peinture. 466p. ill. Paris, Confluences, 1945. *Includes section by Pignon.*

GERTZ, ULRICH. Plastik der Gegenwart. 224p. ill. Berlin, Rembrandt, 1953. *Major section on contemporary German sculpture.*

GIEDION-WELCKER, CAROLA. Contemporary Sculpture: an Evolution in Volume and Space. (Fall release). New York, Wittenborn, 1955. *Notes on Armitage, Butler, Chadwick, Hajdu, Minguzzi, Mirko, Richier and Uhlmann.*

HAFTMANN, WERNER. Malerei im 20. Jahrhundert. 560p. ill. Munich, Prestel, 1954. *"5. Buch: Europäische Gegenwart, Die Kunst der Nachkriegszeit."*

DAS KUNSTWERK (Periodical). Abstrakte Kunst: Theorien und Tendenzen. 132p. ill. Baden-Baden, Klein, 1951. *Reissue of no.8–9, 1950. Includes article on Uhlmann. Bibliography.*

LEBEL, ROBERT, ed. Premier Bilan de l'Art actuel, 1937–1953. Paris, Le Soleil Noir, 1953. *"Le Soleil Noir. Positions. No.3 & 4, 1953."*

MARCHIORI, GIUSEPPE. Pittura moderna in Europa (da Manet à Pignon). 176p. ill. Venezia, Pozza, 1950.

MARTINELLI, VALENTINO. Sculture moderne all'aperto. *Commentari* 4no.4:306–317 ill. Oct.–Dec. 1953. *Reviews major outdoor exhibitions in Europe.*

RITCHIE, ANDREW C. Sculpture of the Twentieth Century. 238p. ill. New York, Museum of Modern Art, 1952. *Includes Butler, Chadwick, Uhlmann and others.*

TATE GALLERY, LONDON. The Unknown Political Prisoner: [24]p. plus insert ill. London, Lund Humphries, 1953. *Sponsored by the Institute of Contemporary Arts. References to Butler, Mirko, Chadwick, Minguzzi.*

TRIER, EDUARD. Moderne Plastik: Von Auguste Rodin bis Marino Marini. 104p. ill. Frankfurt am Main, Gutenberg, 1955. *Includes Butler, Richier, Uhlmann and others.*

XXᵉ SIÈCLE (PARIS). June 1951–current. *New series edited by G. di San Lazzaro. No.1: "Nouveau destins de l'art."—2: "Nouvelles conceptions de l'espace."—3: "Art et poésie depuis Apollinaire."—4: "Rapport sur l'art figuratif."*

NATIONAL GROUPS

FRANCE

COMPAGNIE DE L'ART BRUT, PARIS. L'Art brut Préféré aux Arts culturels. [52]p. ill. Paris, Galerie René Drouin, 1949. *Text by Dubuffet.*

COURTHION, PIERRE. Peintres d'Aujourd'hui. 56p. plus 120 pl. Genève, Cailler, 1952. *Includes Bazaine, Pignon and others.*

DERRIÈRE LE MIROIR (PARIS). 1946–current. *De luxe bulletin and catalog of the Galerie Maeght. Special numbers on Richier (no.15), Bazaine (no.23,55–56) and others.*

DUBUFFET, JEAN. Prospectus aux Amateurs de tout Genre. 154p. Paris, Gallimard, 1946.

FRANCASTEL, PIERRE. Nouveau Dessin, Nouvelle Peinture: L'Ecole de Paris. 187p. ill. Paris, Librairie de Medicis, 1946.

GINDERTAEL, R. V. Radical new position of Paris's younger artists. *Art Digest* 28:15–17, 35 ill. Apr. 15, 1954.

HUYGHE, RENÉ. La Peinture actuelle. 68p. ill. Paris, Tisné, 1945.

LIMBOUR, GEORGES. . . . . L'Art brut de Jean Dubuffet. 103p. ill. New York, Pierre Matisse, 1953. *Bibliography.*

MAEGHT, AIMÉ. Jean Bazaine. 100p. ill. Paris, Editions Maeght, 1953. *Also German, French text. Statements by the artist. Bibliography.*

MOE, HENRIK. Manessier. *Kunsten Idag* 32 no.2:8–27 ill. 1952.

Painting in Paris. *Magazine of Art* 43:169–181 ill. May 1950. *"A discussion of trends by six French critics."*

READ, HERBERT. Edouard Pignon. *The Arts (London)* no.1:4–11 ill. 1948.

SELZ, PETER. Younger French painters of today. *College Art Journal* 11 no.1:10–17 Fall 1951.

SEUPHOR, MICHEL. Etienne Hajdu. ill. Paris, Presses Littéraires de France, 1950.

STAHLY, FRANÇOIS. Die junge französische Plastik. *Werk* 39 no.11:369–376 ill. Nov. 1952.

ZODIAQUE (Periodical). Sens de l'Art moderne: Enquête. 2 parts Paris, Atelier du Coeur-Meutry, 1954. *Special cahiers, 4 no.18–19, Jan. 1954. Includes Bazaine, Manessier and others.*

GERMANY

DOCUMENTS (Periodical). German Contemporary Art. 106p. ill. Offenburg in Baden, Dokumente-Verlag, 1952. *Special edition of "Documents, revue mensuelle des questions allemandes." French and German version, 1951.*

DOMNICK, OTTOMAR, ed. Die schöpferischen Kräfte in der abstrakten Malerei: ein Zyklus. 134p. ill. Bergen, Müller & Kiepenheuer, 1947. *Includes Winter and others.*

GROTE, LUDWIG. Deutsche Kunst im zwanzigsten Jahrhundert. 2. Aufl. 151p. ill. Munich, Prestel, 1954.

HAFTMANN, WERNER. Fritz Winter: 12 Farbtafeln. 18p. plus 12 pl. Bern, Marbach, 1951. *Includes text by Winter. Also note "Profile of Fritz Winter" by J. A. Thwaites in Arts Digest, Oct. 1, 1954.*

KESTNER-GESELLSCHAFT. [Exhibition Catalogs]. Hannover, 1916–current. *Comprehensive coverage of modern artists in Germany, including Werner, Winter, Uhlmann and others.*

LEHMANN-HAUPT, HELLMUT. Art Under a Dictatorship. 277p. ill. New York, Oxford, 1954. *Art in Germany, before, during, and after the Nazi era.*

TÜBINGEN. UNIVERSITÄTS-BIBLIOTHEK. Theodor Werner. [12]p. ill. 1951. *Later exhibited, with variant catalogs, at Franke Gallery (Munich), Möller Gallery (Cologne). Texts by the artist, C. Linfert, C. Zervos, W. Grohmann. Last essay also included in Borgenicht Gallery catalog, New York, 1955.*

WEIDLER, CHARLOTTE. Art in western Germany today. *Magazine of Art* 44:132–137 ill. Apr. 1951.

GREAT BRITAIN

ALLOWAY, LAWRENCE. Nine Abstract Artists: Their Work and Theory. 56p. ill. London, Tiranti, 1954. *Includes Scott and others.*

ALLOWAY, LAWRENCE. Britain's new iron age. *Art News* 52:18–20, 68–70 ill. June 1953. *Also note his: Non-figurative art in England 1953. "Arti Visive" no.6–7 1954.*

English sculptors at Venice. *Architectural Review* 112:129–130 ill. Aug. 1952.

GAUNT, WILLIAM. Art in Britain, 1935–1955. *Arts Digest* 29 no.10:10–12, 22 ill. Feb. 15, 1955.

HODIN, J. P. Testimonianza sulla scultura inglese attuale. *Sele Arte* 2 no.9:57–64 ill. Nov.–Dec. 1953.

IRONSIDE, ROBIN. Painting since 1939. *In Since 1939.* p.145–181 London, Phoenix, 1948. *Originally a British Council brochure.*

MELVILLE, ROBERT. Francis Bacon. *Horizon* 20 no.120–121: 419–423 ill. Dec. 1949–Jan. 1950.

MELVILLE, ROBERT. Personages in iron; work of Reg Butler. *Architectural Review* 108:147–151 ill. Sept. 1950. *Also review of Butler exhibition, Apr. 1954.*

SORRELL, MARY. Mobiles of Lynn Chadwick. *Studio* 144:76–79 ill. Sept. 1952.

THWAITES, JOHN A. Notes on some young English sculptors. *Art Quarterly* 15 no.3:234–241 ill. 1952.

ITALY

ARTI VISIVE (ROME). 1952–current. *"Rivista della Fondazione 'Origine'." Includes Capogrossi, Burri, Mirko and others.*

BRANDI, CESARE. Su alcuni giovani. *Le Arti* 1 no.3:287–293 ill. Feb.–Mar. 1939. *Includes Afro, Mirko and others.*

CAIROLA, STEFANO, ed. Arte Italiana del Nostro Tempo. 130p. plus 104pl. Bergamo, Instituto Italiano d'Arte Grafiche, 1946. *Includes Afro, Minguzzi, Mirko and others.*

CARRIERI, RAFFAELE. Pittura, Scultura d'Avanguardia in Italia (1890–1950). 345p. ill. Milano, Conchiglia, 1950. *Extensive bibliography.*

GENDEL, MILTON. Burri makes a picture. *Art News* 53 no.8: 28–31, 67–69 ill. Dec. 1954.

MARCHIORI, GIUSEPPE. Scultura Italiana Moderna. 48p. plus 36 pl. Venezia, Alfieri, 1953. *English summary. Includes Mirko and others.*

SEUPHOR, MICHEL. Capogrossi. 8p. plus 20 pl. Venezia, Cavallino, 1954. *Italian, French, English text. Also essay in XXᵉ Siècle, no.4:78 Jan. 1954.*

SOBY, JAMES T. & BARR, ALFRED H., JR. Twentieth-Century Italian Art. 144p. ill. New York, Museum of Modern Art, 1949.

VENTURI, LIONELLO. Afro. *Commentari* 5 no.3:245–252 ill. July–Sept. 1954. *Bibliography. Also briefly in his "Otto Pittori" (Rome, De Luca, 1952).*

THE NETHERLANDS

DOTREMONT, CHRISTIAN. Karel Appel. Brussels, Bibliothèque de Cobra, 1950.

This book was printed in April 1955 for the Trustees of the Museum of Modern Art by Connecticut Printers, Inc., Hartford, Connecticut

Designed by Edward L. Mills
Cover designed by Alvin Lustig